DEAR QUAD

'The last of my lovely boys walked out of my life today.' Who are these lovely boys? They are the 'quads', the author's extended family of four-legged creatures — her horses. Sonia Roberts journeys back through her life to the Second World War when she was evacuated to Devon, to her marriage and through her farming career. In her earlier days milking was done by hand and horses played a vital role in the farm's operation. We see the reality of the backbreaking work. And we get an insight into the unique world of horse care and breeding.

SONIA D. ROBERTS

◆

DEAR QUAD

Complete and Unabridged

ULVERSCROFT
Leicester

British Library CIP Data

Roberts, Sonia D.
    Dear quad.—Large print ed.—
    Ulverscroft large print series: non-fiction
    1. Roberts, Sonia D. 2. Women farmers—England—
    Devon—Biography 3. Farmers—England—Devon
    —Biography 4. Country life—England—Devon—
    History — 20th century 5. Large type books
    6. Devon (England)—Biography
    I. Title
    942.3'5085'092

    ISBN 1–84617–367–1

Published by
F. A. Thorpe (Publishing)
Anstey, Leicestershire

Set by Words & Graphics Ltd.
Anstey, Leicestershire
Printed and bound in Great Britain by
T. J. International Ltd., Padstow, Cornwall

This book is printed on acid-free paper

For my dear husband,
Alan,
who has supported me in my aspirations
in the fifty-five years of our marriage,
and
Gill Kenyon,
who put in a great deal of time to
present my manuscript.

List of Photographs

Prologue

The last of my lovely boys walked out of my life today. This, I must clarify, is not one of my two strapping sons, or my long-suffering husband of some forty-five years, but our extended family of quads, as my dear childhood friend, Harry Torduff, used to describe my equines. Harry, my mentor in the field of equine adornment, lived in retirement from a lifetime of service with the 'nobs' quads, in a small Victorian semi in urban Guildford, with a useful outbuilding in the garden stocked up to the hilt with second-hand tack for sale, carefully covered up with immaculate summer sheets, under which occasionally peeped out the shafts of a sometime elegant carriage.

The boys were in fact our many lovely stallions of diverse breeds and types, who lived with us over a period of thirty-five years of our married life, contributing a pretty modest income in fiscal terms, but inestimable job satisfaction in the lovely foals they sired for us together with their animal wisdom generously imparted to us — their slaves — in return for the love and respect we

1

had for them. Today was the end of an era — the break-up of our stud after a lifetime service in my case, to equine and bovine care.

I collect a lead rope and set off up the steep hill field approach to the railed stallion paddock, over the ramparts of what we believe to be a prehistoric earthwork, with its fantastic view over the Bristol Channel into Wales. Elite, the last of the boys detaches himself from the low sward of sweet permanent grass, and benignly ambles towards me. At a little over sixteen hands, he is a 'butty' compact type of Cleveland Bay entire, with a quality head and very large intelligent eyes, which he transmits to his stock. We bred his dam many years ago and selling her to a Yorkshire breeder, bought him from her as a yearling ten years ago.

As I call him, puffing and rather lame from the exertions of my climb, he surveys me keenly, noting my weakness, as I noted his, when nursing him back from an appalling injury, sustained when indulging in high jinks in his steep field, when a neighbour drove some loose mares past his field. Together we descend to the yard where I will have to give him a good strap (groom) to clear the evidence of his rolling excesses, in his favourite hollows in the ancient site.

Philip, my eldest son, is coming with a

lorry to take him back to his yard and prepare him for a five-thousand-mile journey to his new life. First flying him to New York where he will have an initial forty-eight hours' quarantine and thence to three weeks' full quarantine at Baltimore (the USA insists on a very full quarantine and at this time, trial matings with two quarantine mares, to check fertility and freedom from infectious disease). Thence to Idlehour stud in Pennsylvania to join three of our Rambler's-bred Cleveland Bay stallions and colts, living with Tom and Marilyn Webster, for whom we selected some British pure-bred Cleveland fillies last spring. Tom and Marilyn have Rambler's Renown who we sold to Lady Townshend twelve years ago, to go out to her Arabian stud in Virginia to breed international standard driving horses. After Lady Townshend's death he started a new life, Marilyn training him for dressage and jumping and even competing him at the Lexington Trials. He is a dearly loved member of their family, and Elite's new owner will train at the Webster's for a year to learn the intricacies of the breeding game before they move on to a new life together.

More than twenty-five years ago our eldest son was taken very ill necessitating constant care and surveillance, albeit covert. Alan and I subsequently had to part with our two

3

lovely hunters, but in order to allay withdrawal symptoms from the sport we both love, we decided that we would interest ourselves in breeding these tough native horses, now on the Rare Breeds Register. Truly as one door closes and so on, it opened up to us a completely new field of interest and dedication to the breed. We registered sixty-four pure-bred Cleveland Bays into the *Stud Book*, but of course we bred many times that number of part-breds. Only one other breeder has to this day registered more pure-breds and that over a much longer time span. The achievement represents many, many cold, dark vigils in the small hours, to deliver strapping great foals, sometimes reluctant to see the light of day, and frequently requiring back-breaking work to stand them up and get them on the teat, early suckling being essential to establishing the digestive system.

Eventually Phil turned up to collect Elite with a borrowed lorry, for the hundred-and-fifty-mile journey back to his yard. My dear boy, his eyes so trustful, his quarters rounded once again after an unsuccessful trial separation at another stud had left him below par, walked quietly into the lorry, never dreaming that he would never see us again. Crying buckets, having dashed into the privacy of the loo, I was alarmed by sounds of the lorry failing to start. All we need at this juncture, I thought bitterly. Eventually the problem was solved and they departed down the narrow twisting Somerset lane, but by then I had grave misgivings for I have second sight over those I care for.

An hour after their departure I had a premonition that something was wrong — later we discovered that it was at this moment the transmission packed up at Taunton, mercifully just short of the motorway, where Phil had managed to get the lorry onto the industrial site. He managed to get his passenger onto some well-grassed verges under the motorway lights, Elite ignoring the traffic. The relief box driver, who had been told to load a stallion in the dark, and was bracing himself for a tricky job, was tickled pink to find a real pussycat, glad to get in out of a cold wind.

We left Ford Farm in the spring of 1994, which was wet and late, and moved off the hill into a partly-converted barn with fourteen acres after Alan's second heart attack, this time, they said, necessitating a triple bypass operation. Fortunately the consultant, Mr Wisheart, considered it an option to keep Alan under supervision at the Bristol Hospital rather than rush into the operation. We also are devotees of the 'If it ain't broke, don't fix it', being farmers. I also had dodged deep-chest surgery by waiting two years for a bed only to have it offered just before our move to Exmoor. Alan's condition miraculously healed itself in the ensuing fifteen years, as did mine also.

At a thousand feet up, on the Brendon Hills in the Exmoor National Park, spring is always three weeks later than in the foothills facing the Quantocks or the Bristol Channel. The best part of Exmoor is the sense of space, freedom and light that you have around you. Here you need to be impervious to rain and force-ten gales; only a fool would fail to dress for the weather (usually a wetsuit), or fail to heat their houses for a full seven months of the year. The really exhilarating sensation is the keen, clean winds blowing over the fantastic scenery, with the wild moorland as a backdrop to fertile, emerald-coloured grass, more heavily stocked with sheep and cattle than any other place I have seen.

Ford Farm, our semi-retirement home of a comfortable bungalow and fifty acres of excellent grass, accommodated the remains of our stud: sic. two Cleveland Bay stallions, nine mares, two foals and four registered Border collie bitches and one incipient stud

6

dog born the same year as we moved. It was the most fertile farm we have ever owned, and during our stay there, we grazed sometimes forty suckler cows and calves, and two hundred couples, (that is, ewes and lambs) during the summer, besides visiting mares and our own youngstock, as well as making our own hay requirements in the early years.

We moved down from the Home Counties where we had run a stud for more than twenty years, discreetly grading-up properties to make them saleable units in a rapidly expanding equine business market, for alas, smallholding or stud farming on very limited capital is only just viable for a hard-working family, with their sights set firmly at ground level. The property changes allowed us extra capital to improve our living conditions and build up pedigree stock, but as we did most of the building improvements ourselves, alongside our farming activities, it was very hard work, particularly as we were careful to see that we operated on only one property at a time, our own home, or we should be caught for heavy taxes.

The difficulty was that improving property, with enough land to be called a farm, became scarcer and scarcer in the West Surrey-Hampshire borders. We were reluctant to move away, and possibly lose our stud trade; without visiting mares, our stallions would not be properly assessed by their progeny, and the income from visiting mares was helpful in building up our own pedigree Cleveland Bay stud, enabling us to show our youngstock at the National shows, and then sell the stock on well, to get the stallions known internationally.

By the time we were in our sixties, both sons and their families were living in the Exmoor area, and we were becoming dependent on outside help on the stud. With our expanding herd of South Devon cattle, we were missing the help of tough young men, to help us calve-down big cows, bring straw in for the winter, and help with the farm machinery. The young people of the Home Counties were very disinclined to squander their skills in farm duties, or mucking out and caring for horses, although they would consent to grace our yard if they could bring their own eventer or showjumper with them, and have the use of our lorry and the time off to compete.

For once in our life we got it right and in 1987 sold our Elizabethan farmhouse and American-type barn with its dry, sandy in-bye fields for the winter and acres of grassy river-meadows beside the River Wey, on which cattle and horses thrived, just as the housing-market peaked in Surrey, and before the ever-widening ripples of housing inflation reached Somerset. The stay in this lovely property had been short, not only through health difficulties but also Tudor beams had wreaked havoc upstairs, to both of us with second Elizabethan dimensions, resulting in me having knocked myself out so regularly in my domestic duties, that I saw snow in the air even in summer!

Moving had necessitated selling Bladon, our thoroughbred stallion, but in retirement albeit 'semi' we had to reduce our commitment. This meant dispersing our lovely South Devon herd, a great sadness to me. My sons said, 'If you are going to retire, then leave the cattle behind.' Good advice but hard to stomach. In the event our new purchaser took on a nucleus of the herd including our pride and joy, King Kong — the big daddy of them all, our other stock sold locally, and it is a great pleasure to us now to see a really large population of South Devons in our old stamping grounds, many having emanated from our foundation stock.

In the early sixties, with any luck, you still have enough energy and drive left for fresh starts to be made with enthusiasm, so eventually we were on the road to the West, our horse stock incarcerated in two huge hired lorries, our stallions in our own, plus furniture lorry, two cars, one pulling a trailer with stable equipment, the other with five dogs and two cats. The John Deere tractor and other farm machinery, having gone on separately, on a low-load was unable to get to an unloading quay anywhere near the farm, because of the narrow, twisting lanes, and was stuck at Williton which eventually involved driving it all up to the rarified air of the Brendons at a thousand feet altitude.

We arrived to the mundane task of getting yet another stud farm organised. The nine mares obviously fed up with their long journey in a strange lorry, hightailed it round the new fields, which despite my entreaties to the vendor, had been stripped to the bone (of grass) by agisted sheep and which in mid-September looked as if they would never grow again. Actually within a month they had fully recovered. Our youngest son George, the builder, had nearly completed the addition to an existing machinery shed, which gave us six big loose boxes around a 60 by 30 feet exercising area, all under one roof, which was to prove a real boon at this altitude. The Border collies were always perfectly happy as long as they had livestock for them to watch over, and were put in a loose box whilst their kennels were under construction. The two cats were quite unruffled as long as we, the dogs and the stallions, were about in the yard, although they had howled like banshees in their baskets for the whole way down.

As we had only one paddock suitable for the stallions to start with, the boys had to go out in turn for exercise. The senior boy, Wiscombe Arthur, I had ridden regularly under saddle in Surrey. Top of the peck-order he had the biggest and best stallion stable with a fine view over the house and paddocks. Artie had his ego massaged by being told he was the greatest, although he was knocking on a bit. Even if time was short for the customary afternoon strap (groom), we made sure that there was always time to stop for a chat to him as we passed his box. He had the best accommodation and knew it, glancing triumphantly at Elite next door, when taken out for first turn-out.

It had been impossible to turn him out in the Farnham area as he could pop over the most enormous fences effortlessly if he heard some mares in the distance. Here he had to learn new ways; with such steep fields and banks to the paddocks jumping out would be fatal. Daily his time out was increased. When we were wanting him, Jen, our best working bitch who had been waiting eagerly for this, was given the nod and unassisted ran to the top of his field five hundred yards away, to persuade him to come down to the gate to wait for us to collect him, which she could do without noise or teeth by giving him the collie 'strong eye'. Elite went out on the afternoon shift, but had a change by going into the 'school' or another box in the mornings.

Those first winter months ahead of us at Ford, meant a lot of work to organise accommodation for us all, but to sweeten the pill we had two Cleveland mares we had left empty, so we could enjoy some fox-hunting over this wonderful rural landscape before we had to hang up our boots for good. The next eight years of semi-retirement were very sweet. Although the journeys to the shows were much longer, we still continued to get to the Royal Show and even to Ascot for the Southern Show. It meant an early start before dawn and as we climbed up from our sheltered farm to the top of the escarpment of the Brendon Hills, the whole of the coastline from Watchet to Weston-Super-Mare was laid out in front of us on a fine day, sparkling with a myriad of town lights and whilst Exmoor remained dark, the Welsh coastline was also lit up for our inspection, the other side of the Bristol Channel.

One time Alan and I, failing to get a

yearling colt loaded in the dark, looked across our quiet farm to see our neighbours lambing sheds ablaze with lights where our neighbour was busy with his lambing vigil. In no time he came down with us and gave the necessary shove to get us on our way. Rambler's Lottie, one of our famous Lee family, had started her showing career in 1986 at the Royal where she was first prize foal and her mother, Lee, Reserve Breed Champion. The following year she herself was First in her class and Reserve Breed Champion.

In 1988 and for the next three years she was Breed Champion at the Royal for us when she was bought by Sir John Miller to go to the Hampton Court stud. The following year she came back to us to visit Elite, and Alan won a fourth Breed Championship at the Royal with her before we delivered her back to the royal stud where she was now the property of HM The Queen. She went on to win several more championships there in the royal ownership.

Her sister, Leonie, another Royal Show Champion, was also purchased to go to the royal stud. It was a proud time for us when having organised a parade of Cleveland Bays at Dunster Castle Country Fair, HM The Queen sent down two Rambler's mares Leah, (another Lee daughter) and Lucky Miss, to parade, driven to the Balmoral Sociable, a favourite carriage of Queen Victoria. The driving horses stayed with us and enjoyed the luxury of stretching in deep straw beds for their night-time rest as they had stalls at home. We so enjoyed seeing the staff; the Head Coachman had come down with them. The staff enjoyed a few days of Somerset hospitality, and the weather was grand for them. The parades at Dunster were always a great success with so many people interested in the grand old British breed; sponsored by a local feed business it was a real country occasion.

Book One

1

As you look back over a lifetime certain signposts mark the way you travelled. The Second World War was one of the most significant of these for me. Pre-war, I was a school child, always mad on ponies. This was not a social status as it is today. I was called 'Old Horsey' at school; it was not a flattering epithet and I can only recall two other girls at Guildford High who rode at all. My family was urban, and their interests were literary, artistic and musical. The youngest of three, by eight and ten years, I made my own amusements and perhaps the event I recall, opened my eyes to the heights of equine attainment, was when one of the regional agricultural shows, visited Stoke Park before the war and I looked over the fence of our playing fields, to see these beautifully turned-out, magic combinations, competing at the highest level, in showing and jumping classes.

Compared to the little hairy native ponies that grazed the river meadows below our house in the Great Quarry, and that I fed and cared for and rode out for their benevolent owner, the landlord of the Seven Stars public house Guildford, these were on another planet. I studied their beautifully plaited manes and tails, and their, to my eyes, complicated and unaccustomed tack, their miraculously white socks and stockings, and water-brushed quarter markings with brightly checked sheets to cover the horses' quarters when their stylishly clad riders came out of the ring. I did not cycle home from games that day until very late. This event left an indelible mark on my unsophisticated mind; one day I would have horses of my own like that, however long it took.

It did take a very long time because war broke out and I was sent to Devon, my birthplace, to be evacuated, staying with Exeter acquaintances, who probably thought I was a better bet, certainly financially, than the trainloads of East Enders who were arriving daily, labels in their lapels, to be placed in a safer environment than the city. My hosts, living in a delightful Regency residence in their own parkland, had a nice quality hunter for their daughters' use, which I privately thought too thin, despite its aristocratic lines. I was not invited to ride it.

I had always loved Devon having spent wonderful summer holidays, staying on my own with a farming family my parents knew at Tipton St John, near Ottery St Mary. Travelling down alone at the age of ten from Waterloo on the South Western Railway, the compartments of which carried the most unflattering views of Weston-Super-Mare, Sidmouth, Budleigh Salterton and similar watering places in faded sepia tone. I was usually under the eye of the guard, who found me a place near a suitable elderly lady chaperon, (my mother had great faith in the railways — her family having been something big in the LSW). My great adventure was changing trains at Sidmouth junction on to the little Sidmouth Line. Here I was usually on my own and greatly concerned because when the train pulled in at Tipton St John, my destination, the tiny platform did not extend to my coach! Leaning out in some alarm the Station Master told me benignly: 'Don't worry, my dear, us'll get you there directly.' Then with another puff of smoke, and a few more clanks, the engine driver got me spot on, and I was helped out in real style by the porter, eventually discovering my host Harold Thomas and his ancient coupe-style automobile ready to take me home to Fluxton, a short distance up the road.

Fluxton was a magic place: a wonderful seventeenth-century longhouse farm, with a tiny stream which came past the dairy window, keeping the slate flagstones and shelves cool in the hottest summers. The many ducks could be seen floating past the window as you looked out: 'Ducks down a dabbling up tails all' as I used to recite when I was small. Hilda Thomas who sadly had no children of her own, made all the butter and cream there, and gladly showed me the intricacies of hand-churning, clotted cream and butter making, hand-separating and patting-up, and stamping the pats for market.

The house was extended in the typical West Country fashion so that the eldest son of the family also resided in one part of the house, with semi-retired parents comfortably ensconced in the rest of the farmhouse. Even with two families in occupation there was masses of room, as apart from a huge kitchen there was an equally large back kitchen, which had no doubt housed the beasts when the house was first built. Whereas the main kitchen had a mighty iron range, the back Inglenook open fire was fuelled with faggots from hedge-laying activities, and here all the separated milk was left in buckets by the fire to warm up for the calves, a handful of mineral additive being added before feeding.

Young lambs were rescued weak from the lambing pens and kept before the fire in boxes here, and bottle-fed if they could not be fostered elsewhere. Naturally, wet sheep-dogs also stole in to dry off, eggs washed, poultry mash mixed, a very large slate trough and hand pump supplying all water for both kitchens under a lean-to on the side of a little flagged yard with all the domestic outbuildings surrounding it. Here Hilda's more treasured broods of fancy hens and ducks were reared, as although the main gates to the yard were kept closed, there was a hole in the yard wall for them to free range outside and use the stream.

Having done service to the domestic part of the farm, as well as watering the upper fields, the stream went through a hole in the fence — well wired to keep the poultry out — and tinkled merrily across the front lawn where it ran in well-tamed grassy banks, subject to Harold's weekly mowing. Diverted through a stone wall it then ran through a couple of granite troughs in successive yards, and was then piped under the road to water the lower meadows which ran down to the River Otter. It was a veritable marvel of rural water management and we found this also when later in life we farmed in Somerset, where the tiniest streams were harnessed to power mills for engineering and food production. In the eighteenth century no less than thirteen mills used the power of the tiny

Roadwater River for the benefit of the village. The ingenuity in the placing of the leats to convey water to these is fascinating, and leads one to wonder why we now rely on expensive electricity when there is so much buckshee water in the West.

Visits to Fluxton included the use of the senior Mr Thomas's sixteen-hand hunter mare, Kitty. Her owner — then an octogenarian — would clamber aboard with his crook in his hand to go round the farm and check the stock. Kitty would wait quietly tied to a fence or a gate while he hobbled around them; then he usually found a gate or a bank to help him mount. During my holidays I was given Kitty to go round the farm with him, whilst he rode a fairly unpredictable liver-chestnut mare called Curry, which his son, Harold, hunted. The stock-round over the fairly bare hill fields at the back of the farm, included taking bags of feed for the lambs across the saddles, and cutting and tying enough of the standing crop of the old-fashioned horse clover, for the bull and three workhorses' lunch. This again was hoisted over the saddles.

Free-range chicken houses were checked, heads counted but egg collecting left to the indomitable Hilda, who struggled up later in the day. In the afternoons I was summoned by Harold to help get the South Devon herd in for milking. The two hunters rested in their stable by day, out of the summer flies. I was able to get a bridle on trustworthy Kitty on my own, hardly strong enough to girth up the saddle, so standing her alongside the low brick wall of the midden in the centre of the cattle yard, she allowed me to struggle up unaided, and follow Harold down to the water meadows to call up the matrons of this wonderful dual-purpose breed, the more sluggish enjoying the sweet tussocks in the wetter areas and needing considerable urging, bareback contact with the mare quite comfortable in her well-padded summer condition.

The yard buildings at Fluxton were a veritable treasure trove. The store sheds by the pump housed a jumble of bygones which would nowadays gladden the heart of any auctioneer. At that time it was a repository for anything which might one day be of use. In earlier centuries farm workers lined up in the morning for the day's cider ration, which was one of their perks having been concerned in its manufacture from the home orchard fruit, milled in the ancient granite horse-powered cider crush. This was dispensed into their own miniature barrel called a firkin. It had a bung and a carrying strap made of a leather bootlace, which went out to the fields with them. When farming was prospering this was a half-gallon measure, but alas! later on in a farming recession, half-sized firkins came into use. The staff were so incensed about this, that when they arrived back from the fields after a particularly hot spell during harvesting, when the juices had run dry, instead of placing the firkins carefully in the cider shed for filling in the morning, they hurled them furiously against the back wall, where many of the broken firkins, too damaged to mend, lay about forlornly still.

Old seed fiddles were for sowing grass, before the more modern shandy barrow which in wartime I trundled like a wheel barrow, when the Eytie prisoners of war, broke off for lunch. Horses and men could stop for lunch but not land girls! There were chaff-cutters, winnowing machines for cleaning seed corn, cow-cake crushers, broody-hen breakers, chick runs and feeders interspersed with the articles I was sent to find. Sinister little bottles of sheep medicine for anointing, bigger ones of red and brown fluid for bloat in cattle and sheep, and of course Tippers Mystery Salts, which needed a good dose of the farmer's personal faith, to expect results in the more bizarre conditions in cattle.

The old cider-mill was in perfect condition,

a little circular roof on top of the press, where the apples and straw were made into a cheese, the granite circular trough below catching the juice as it spurted out under the pressure caused by the horse-gear as it screwed the press down ever tighter. Beware of the raw juice before fermentation! Its effects could be disastrous on the human stomach, which in the days of water supplies in close proximity to cattle yards, were a great deal tougher than today.

Through this little kingdom Hilda ran a few special fowls, with interesting pedigrees with their own cockerels; these made the contented talking noises of happy hens, so seldom seen or heard today. Amongst them were diverse breeds of ducks and geese, and an immense collection of cats, which waited for the calves' feed buckets to be carried for their twice daily rations. The shiny well-scoured steel-coated milking and carrying buckets were stored in the back kitchen, but the villainous tiny, short legged milking stools, made for a race of dwarfs, and as old as the hills, were kept in the primitive cow shed, only the hurricane lamps lived on the back kitchen table, together with the house oil lamps. These required regular daily filling and trimming, and the older Victorian lamps were lovingly polished and cast a wonderful soft glow in the living rooms, completely masking any deficiencies in the decor.

At six in the morning in my little room over the kitchen, I was awakened by Harold carrying out the many buckets to the cow yard, juggling with hurricane lamps when it was dark which it usually was in the shippon which had no windows or white paint. He and his chap having tied up all the cows in their wooden stalls, I was encouraged to come out and learn to milk. South Devon cows are the largest breed of cattle in the country; they also have the largest and toughest teats to pull. Given a bucket and stool and directed to an old trusty, I was initiated into this ancient art. A satisfactory sound of methodical swishing and pinging of Harold and his stockman into empty buckets merely served to underline my own fumbling efforts to raise a stream of milk, whilst trying to fold up long legs to grip a bucket, whilst the three legged stool, worn to only five inches of leg, most of that having gone to ground in the deep straw permanently carpeting the ancient shippon.

I suspect now that I was only given the drying-off cows to practise on; certainly it taught me to hand-milk fast and efficiently, as the suckler calves were released from their pens after we had taken what milk was needed that day for processing, to empty the udders and get their own rations. The South Devon was always a dual-purpose breed (many farmers today wish this was still the case instead of having been turned into yet another beef breed) so as well as producing a lot of high butterfat milk, they also produce very good beef and strong, quick maturing calves. They are very calm, gentle cattle, but one day at Fluxton I had a nasty surprise.

All the original West Country buildings had a tallet over; this area served as a hay and straw store, and the floor just in front of the cattle mangers was left open so that fodder could be thrown down directly into the mangers. In the original old buildings, the tallet was floored by saplings, and thin tree branches laid across them, bracken and brushwood laid on top to make it fairly impervious, and approached by an outside ladder against the wall. This was my favourite quiet rendezvous with the cat population, as facing south, with no front wall, it was a sunny cosy spot much loved by the cats, who raised numerous families in it. Looking for kittens one day, I moved further along the tallet than ever before. Suddenly my left leg went through the floor up to my thigh.

Looking through a crack I saw the huge

South Devon bull, weighing nearly a ton or so, viewing my leg which was dangling level with his back. The poor chap was permanently incarcerated except when allowed out for business, and was eyeing me in an unmistakably hostile manner, eyes red and popping, and pistol-like snorts emitting from his nostrils. With no one about in the yards at this time, I had the greatest difficulty in extricating myself from this near squeak, without falling through altogether. I did not go up again that holiday!

The memories which will stay with me for ever of those early days on the Devon farm, are of waking in my cosy room under the eaves, on a foggy August morning and hearing the bellowing of the cows in the yards outside, interspersed by masculine shouts, as adjacent farmers tried to separate two identical herds of south Devon cows all horned, which had broken down their boundary fence in the night and fraternised in one group. Another was the very special smell of the *Farmer and Stockbreeder* newspaper which I read from cover to cover as soon as Harold had finished with it.

The house itself had the special smell of an old house, carefully maintained, of apple wood log fires, oil lamps and shelves full of slightly musty boys' books, which Harold and his father had collected: *Stalky and Co.*, and *Eric, or Little by Little*, which I waded through in the tallet one summer. Hilda's home-made lemonade was nectar — nothing like it have I ever tasted since!

2

The Phoney war which had precipitated the evacuation of so many children, dragged on and on. As I was missing education and my home, not to speak of my pony activities sponsored by mine host of the Seven Stars, Guildford (many years later to be the scene of an appalling terrorist attack). This gentleman as well as owning a little farm at Lady Mead — now under an enormous industrial complex — also owned a field beside the River Wey under the ancient quarry in which we lived, and in which an assortment of young ponies grazed, with his permission I and some friends visited these after school and in no time they were quiet enough for us to ride.

Leaving them had been very hard and so my return back to Guildford and school was anticipated with some relief, only to find on arrival that the school had had another evacuated to it and that my classroom appeared to have toddlers' furniture allocated to it, which to a tall fourteen year old was the bottom. Education seemed to have been totally disrupted, with gas-mask drill in the shelters. Blackout precautions ruled our lives. In fact it was only after I returned home that the first air raids occurred and we had to retire to our shelter which my father and brother-in-law had built, dug into the wooded slopes in our garden under the towering chalk quarry, which was worked in Roman times.

My brother was in the Army having finished at Oxford, my father in the Home Guard, my sister, her husband now away on war service, was living at home working for a bank, and fire-watching at night. My mother was doing Red Cross work. In the summer holidays of 1940 I managed to persuade a local farmer to take me on for a holiday job. The driver of the pony and milk float had been injured — I discovered only later that the mare had run away in town with the empty churns, having delivered the milk to the dairies and run into the stone wall of St Mary's Church in Quarry Street.

The mare, a sharp Welsh Cob, was a little cracker! About 14.2 hands high, she and I took a liking to each other. I looked after her in the nag stables, close to the Georgian manor farmhouse: Georgian fanlights over the door and a good well, set in the cobbles at the entrance door, no electricity. The working horse stables being a long way down the hierarchy were at the sharp end of the farm, between the cow sheds and the horse pond, so had no well of their own and heavily cobbled, not paved floors.

Getting Dolly tacked up was always rather a struggle; to fit really well a working collar needs to be fairly tightly stuffed, because unlike a carriage horse, the mare had to pull heavy loads on sometimes heavy, muddy fields. Her collar did not open as some do, but had to be shoved on in a pear shape, and then reversed around the gullet and drawn down to rest on her chest. Usually the heims and traces were left attached. Dolly was always very cooperative about this and getting the bridle on was easy. She was turned in her stall to face me for this, the pad, circingle, crupper and breeching having been put on whilst the mare was tied to her manger. Then taking her outside, the shafts were held up whilst she reversed to command beneath them, when they were lowered the traces being hooked back to the float and the balance girth keeping the shafts to the correct height for her, fastened.

I had one of the heavy horsemen to show me how to do this for a day or two. Arthur was a tiny wiry little Norfolk horseman, from a family with eleven children. He had been looking after the mare himself after the demise of her previous driver so I was able to do the milk run with him for a day or two until he gave the okay to the boss. He and the other horseman habitually carried two-hundredweight sacks of barley up the steep steps to the granary, and from the rear view, only his boots and gaiters and a pair of hands could be seen under this heavy load. With his lilting Norfolk accent he told me 'Look Gel, good things be wrapped in small parcels!' — I was always 'The Gel' to the twelve or so workers on this 200-acre mixed farm.

Dear Dolly and I had some wonderful times — first the sharp trot into town from Shalford, some three miles and sometimes in heavy frost so cold that the unlucky driver had to get out of the back and run along behind the float holding reins and the back of the float to prevent freezing up completely, then unloading the seven or eight churns of milk into Lymposs and Smees' dairies. These had to be rolled hand over hand into the inner recesses and sterilised churns brought back in their place. Then there was a multitude of shopping items to be collected for the farm. West Surrey Farmers' Association Stores had to be visited for tractor and machinery parts, farm medicines and numerous other items. The pony could not always be trusted to stand patiently with so much going on around her, so a half-hundredweight grain scale weight was taken out of the float and attached to her halter rope. All horses were obliged to wear halters under their bridles as war regulations in case of air raids when their drivers would be forced to take shelter. The standard joke of all farm labourers to a new lad was to send them off for a pair of 'Sky hooks'. Even in my innocence at the age of fifteen, I did feel that this sounded rather suspicious so I ignored this request. Driving home in a drizzle, one of these wags enquired after the sky hooks which would have to be used to get the clouds up again!

Tuesday, market day, I had to get at least one load of fat lambs in after the milk run in early morning. This meant driving across to the other end of the farm to Shep's own particular domain, a three-sided courtyard with his lambing hut handy, and listening to his complaints that they had not sent a stronger chap to help lift the sheep into the float. With a net over these to prevent them jumping out, I went back into town to the market at Dolly's slap-up pace; she would brook no checking except down the slippery cobbles of the lower High Street, where eventually they put traffic lights, the railway's dray horses and Dolly's hind shoes afire with sparks, as the horses braced against the breeching, indeed the only brake available in a float.

When there were no lambs to go, there were usually calves from the thirty head of Shorthorn milking cows in the tender care of my dear old friend, Syd. He was the most assiduous stockman I have ever seen. Incredibly neat and tidy, he had a rather dashing appearance when off-duty, with a racy looking Fedora and a whippet at his side. He was also an avid reader of the *Sporting Times* and much in demand by the other workers before big races. He had a regular little flutter with the Shalford bookmaker, as did most of the men, Syd taking the bets for them. I was introduced to the intricacies of double and treble chances but betting has always left me cold — probably because my mathematics is so bad!

Syd, realising I was a very tall fifteen year old, only an inch short of six feet tall, working pretty hard, used to make sure I had my 'perk' of half a pint of milk, fresh through the cooler, at every evening milking. This had to be consumed on the premises with Syd keeping cavey. Of course all the stockmen took their milk rations home with them in traditional metal cans every night after work so we had a big line of cans to fill.

Syd showed me how to calve and serve the

cows with the big white shorthorn bull, and also to recognise signs of unthriftyness. Hay was cut from the rick in the nearby rickyard, tied with plaited twine which had a hazel toggle at one end divided into trusses of fifty-six pounds, this done by very accurate guessing except when sales were concerned when they had to be weighed on the barn scales brought outdoors for the purpose. These were hauled into the barn by Dolly or the workhorses if they were not out on field cultivation work. There were two teams and an odd horse called the Boy's horse to fill in, in the event of a lame or sick horse or to be attached as an extra to the binder in a difficult harvest when the teams were often overstretched.

There was tremendous competition between the carters to have their teams in peak condition at all times, and quite a few accusations as to the state of their own individual corn bins, carrying the week's ration of oats. Ultimately they padlocked these and kept the keys in their pockets. At the week ends after twelve o'clock Saturday, even if they were not on overtime, they turned up individually, to feed their own teams as usual. When taking the threshed corn to Bottings Mill at Chilworth, both men cleaned their gaiters up after work the night before, giving their teams an extra polish. Arthur determined to get one over Bill, the other horseman, got in an hour earlier in the morning to braid the manes and tails up with bass for their infrequent road trips. Enormous nosebags were always filled in the morning for the midday rest, if the horses were unable to get back to stables then the stop would be somewhere near a trough or ditch with water. At this time although there was a big tractor for field work, the pace of the farm was dictated by horse needs.

No one but a horseman ever fed his team. In the early morning, although hurricane lamps glimmered palely through the half doors, stamping and blowing noises indicated the horses were eating their first feed of the day and were not to be disturbed until the last oat had been prised out of the cracks in the heavy wooden troughs in front of their stalls. Their attendants made themselves busy on other jobs such as carrying hay and mangolds which were always fed with chaff, the horses unlike the cattle, chewing these up themselves, whereas the stationary engine in Syd's barn had numerous highly dangerous leather belts connecting it to various machines such as the grain crusher, and mangold-pulper, a sight these days to give a Safety Officer apoplexy! Although we were always told that mangolds were 95% water, and therefore of little food value, there was no doubt that coats of horses and cows fed on them gleamed as though on a high protein diet. As roots get their nourishment from deep underground I suspect it was the additional minerals obtained in this feed which suited the stock. Certainly the cattle yields always went down when they were omitted, but they were hard work to harvest, clamp up, and tote round.

In the afternoons, although the milkers did not finish up until five o'clock, the horses came in at four p.m. and the horsemen had an hour for evening stables. Working horses came back from the fields, had their bridles removed, and on their own made their way up to the horse pond with collars, pads and chains jingling at their sides, to wade deep into the middle to drink and splash the muddy water over their sweaty bodies. When I attended evening stables, to save drawing up water from the well, I would usually jump on Dolly bareback and trot down to the pond making sure I got her watered before the teams came thundering up, muddying the water. When the horsemen arrived in the morning the teams would once again go out for their drink, breaking the ice if necessary; they did not stop long though queuing up sedately to go through the stable doors to get to their breakfasts in the manger.

The carthorses were very wise. It was never necessary to lead them about. Working horses were trusted to know their jobs and do them with minimal human interference. All horses were tied by their headcollar ropes through the ring in their wooden stall-troughs, a large wooden block at the end of the rope which would not pull through the ring, giving them limited movement in their stalls which were about seven feet wide. The stalls were cleaned every morning and evening, the horses standing on cobbles by day, the extra night straw being raked out from under the manger to make a deep bed for them at night, when they would take their ease on it all night. Quality riding horses and hunters were given exactly the same treatment; only brood mares or racehorses qualified for loose boxes, unless an animal was lame or unfit when there was normally a loose box at the end of the stalls for these emergencies.

The result of this practice was that the horses became much more disciplined from an early age. Accustomed to being tied up or standing in the afternoons in pillar-chains, facing the front, as riding horses were, they could all be left unattended for long periods, essential for carriage horses, and even Dolly who was a really sharp pony would stand unattended in a large field of kale, while I cut enough kale for thirty cows, laid in two rows wide enough for the pneumatic wheels of the float to clear, then at a call she would turn round and daintily walk up the cleared section of the crop, until stopped by voice for loading to begin.

Nowadays people forget the discipline all horses learned when we depended on them for our living. The bakers', and milk-delivery horses acted exactly the same as the milkman, going from house to house collecting and delivering bottles, the horse quietly sticking to the left-hand side, moving up the road to a whistle from his driver. Lymposs and Smee, our large dairy depot in Guildford, had dozens of good looking cobs, their coats gleaming with health, standing sandwiched quite tight in swinging partitions, covered in coconut matting, at their stables.

3

At the end of the summer of 1940 — a vile harvest if I remember rightly, with stooked corn growing out of the ear in unrelenting rain. Dolly and I doing a daily run to collect the greenest and most weedy stooks, for there were no weed sprays in use then, to deliver them to the few hundred free-range hens tended by the daughter of the house.

My return to school looked very imminent; it was clear that I was never going to make the grade as an academic, my whole interest was the land and animal husbandry. I asked my boss if he would keep me on if I could get my parents to agree; he replied, certainly but he did not think I would have any chance of this, and neither did I actually, but life in wartime was topsy-turvy and unbelievably my father agreed I could leave school as I should soon be sixteen, provided I was employed on a proper basis, and had some time off at weekends — this was a period when many stockmen worked seventy hours a week although their pay was based on a sixty hour week and so with the greatest joy I embarked on what I (and he privately) considered the best education for life — full employment and training by a series of good-hearted, kindly, and certainly meticulous farm work-men, at a time when the uncertainties of war loomed over everything, and call up affected every family in the land.

Too young as yet for the Land Army, and still under parental supervision, I, like most of my generation, was certainly not allowed out late at night and in early teens had little interest in boys. We saw the 'forties as a fascinating experience when life was changing rapidly and pre-war values suddenly lost their currency. My boss's elderly widower father lived in the family house, and he had employed land girls in World War I. He was very encouraging to me and had many reminiscences of the work that girls had undertaken for him in that war. In the intervening years the men had come back on the scene and the women had been unwanted in agriculture until war reared its head again. Cycling to the farm in the early morning, a three mile ride, for morning milking at five-thirty on dark winter mornings, the only traffic on the roads would be the bicycles of those either going to work, or returning from night duty at hospital or factory, or from the fire-watching rota. As I had always cycled a similar distance to school, I could manage a good pace, but would frequently find my young boss, reserved from call up, but on night duty with the fire service, would pass me at a tremendous pace, and precede me to the farm, where he hand-milked his allotted eight cows before going to bed for a spell. There were four of us on the early milking, so we only had around eight cows each. In emergency one of the Carters would lend a hand, while the other did the teams (but this would mean handing over the key to his corn-bin, so not very popular).

So life ran on for me on a pretty even keel, as I learned my job. There were about fourteen employed during harvest, which would include several schoolboys, awaiting call up and one or two itinerant labourers, who turned up from time to time. One of these was 'Shortie' who always arrived with a large carpet bag slung on the handlebars of his bike. Every worker used a bike as transport. He was said to be a bit 'quick' and anything that 'disappeared' was likely to be blamed on Shortie: on one occasion, unbelievably, a broody hen and a newly hatched batch of chicks.

All the men who occupied the most charming seventeenth-century cottages, now all turned into gentlemen's residences, had their gardens cultivated into miniature smallholdings and apart from excellent vegetables sprinkled with cottage flowers they had pens of chickens which entailed a lot of swapping with one another's setting eggs and broody hens and there was always one pig which was slaughtered in strict calendar sequence so that after slaughter, all the families on the farm benefited from sweetbreads and other offal delicacies.

Uncle Bill also lived in the farmhouse, which was a handsome building redolent of a previous century's affluence. To Bill was entrusted all the thatching work. Corn stacks were built in an oval shape, thatched up like a farmhouse loaf, in a very neat and enduring fashion, for the sign of an affluent farmer in those days was not an expensive car in the drive, or a private aircraft but a number of corn ricks standing straight as houses, the farmer's capital allowing him to wait until the very end of the winter before threshing these, thus getting the highest prices, not to speak of some good sport with the workers' terriers, for as the thresher ate down to the last few feet of corn, a twelve-inch roll of wire netting was stretched outside the rick and any rats living in the bottom of the stack made a dash to safety. In a badly infested stack a good terrier could kill fifty rats.

Uncle Bill may have been a good thatcher,

but as a crusty old bachelor he was a sore trial to me, as one of my myriad of jobs was to fill up milk churns with water and deliver them wherever he was working on the farm. The water was to enable him to draw the 'reed', that is the long pieces of straw out of the truss, no bales in those days, so old fashioned types of wheat such as 'Little Joss' could be relied upon to produce really long straw which seldom went down in a storm because it received practically no bag fertilizer as the sheep would have been folded over a root crop prior to ploughing, or a green crop such as clover could have been ploughed in for the same purpose.

A lot of water was used on the straw during the process of reed-combing and Uncle Bill was another grumbler like Shep, who would have preferred one of the family to moan at, and my late arrival in the morning after doing a few other jobs first, such as the milk run, farm shopping, lamb and calf marketing, provoked another spate of grumbling at my lateness and a permanent shortage of churns for his use. We used to empty the clean ten-gallon churns from the dairy into several old seventeen-gallon creamery cans that were usually knocking about in Shep's domain. Like most young people straight from school I was so used to being moaned at, that this did not upset me very much though Syd was very sympathetic to me.

I was fascinated to see how each enterprise on the farm, dovetailed into the next. You can depend on it that any straw left over from thatching would be scratched up by me, loaded into the float and carted off to another department to use up! There was no doubt that Dolly and I fulfilled the same purpose as the farmer's pick-up today. Another of the boss's uncles lived in Guildford, and used to swap bee stocks with the 'old man'.

Naturally, this was added to my 'Guildford after the Milk Run' shopping list, and the bees installed amongst the empty churns which were as usual tied tightly up with rope. Within half a mile of my journey home with them, to my horror I saw the bees beginning to leak out of their strong box, and begin buzzing around me and Dolly's hindquarters very angrily. Forsaking the road to get home fast I took to the field path, whipping Dolly up into a fast canter, hoping to lose some on the way home. Lurching from pothole to wheel track in a very dangerous fashion it became all too clear that the bees could easily keep up with us, and they were getting crosser and crosser at the jangling accompaniment to our rough ride. Coming round the corner of the field path to the back of the stables was negotiated on one wheel. I got Dolly to a halt and somehow unhitched her from the float, running her full tilt into her stable and shutting the door tight. A call at the back door of the farmhouse told the family that the next step was theirs and theirs alone!

The enormous farm staffs of those days made pay night a real ritual and could lead to putting in forty minutes' overtime (unpaid) in the wages queue. Dear Syd, who as anxious as an old hen that I should get home to my tea in good time, told me the way to circumnavigate these problems. The boss paid wages at the kitchen table on Friday night and the accepted rule was to wait in a queue outside the back door to go in turn, to sign and receive it along with any special wartime food rations appertaining. A special cheese ration was one extra at harvest and so on 'Now my gel,' he told me 'Just you go in with the family's milk through the back door and into the dairy, then when you hear the one in the queue ahead of you get his money, pop out and say, 'Shall I take my wages now, boss?' That'll work,' and it did for the two years I was there.

As the war progressed, more and more Army traffic was encountered on the roads. Quarry Street which ran tight beside St

Mary's churchyard was particularly narrow. Dolly and I with our very fragile vehicle were squeezed alongside huge tank carriers and all manner of armoured vehicles, which made my lively steed snort and blow with fright. Then a morning came when at morning stables, pitch black with no electricity to lighten the gloom, I lit my hurricane lamp and fork in hand, blearily, opened the door of the loose box adjoining Dolly's stall and stuck my prong deep into some hay for her breakfast, when the unimaginable occurred! The whole box was alive with Canadian soldiers who had dossed down in the hay for the night. As I had no idea that there were troops about the previous evening, I nearly collapsed with shock! They were all in camouflage gear with blackened faces as they were on manoeuvres prior to going out to France and in the fitful light of a hurricane they looked enormous.

As daylight dawned I discovered the whole farm had been taken over by them and a field kitchen installed in a barn. They were the kindest, nicest chaps imaginable and the manoeuvres lasted several days providing more harrowing frights for Dolly as they stepped out from behind trees with rifles and full equipment as we passed on the milk run. When they left I found myself the recipient of all sorts of goodies, candy and nylons which we had not seen for years. They were so generous and I fear they suffered terrible losses in the battles to come.

My parents offered hospitality to visiting troops through the Aldershot Overseas Forces Hospitality Group. We met some charming young lads who had been scooped up from backland farms in Canada and the Midwest. Also we for some while had some super New Zealand lads, who we became very fond of, before they left England to fight in the first invasion of Europe. Here we heard they suffered the most appalling casualties. I believe the New Zealanders were the first to face the enemy guns, the second wave having to advance over the fallen. Every time I hear someone say our ties are now to Europe, I remember these boys who died for us, whilst the French and the Low Countries submitted without a fight. I still pay my particular homage by buying New Zealand butter and lamb for our household.

Folly, doing war service on the farm

Ramblers Farley Green

4

After I had been working for a while I managed to save enough money, after paying my mother a little something for my keep, to buy my first horse, which the boss said I could keep with Dolly in her paddock. What a time to buy a horse! Most of the thoroughbred racing stock slaughtered and gone, riding horses no longer wanted, I found the horse of my dreams in my dear friends', Percy and Ada Podger's, yard. They had a nice little dairy farm outside Godalming and being hunting and racing people, always had a few good hunter types in their dealing yard. A big upstanding bay mare of sixteen hands two inches cost me twenty pounds. A little visit to Harry Torduff (as usual for market days, in buttoned gaiters, shiny boots, with slightly grubby stock under a drab coat and brown bowler). Carefully soaped and covered up with immaculate check summer sheets his stock was enormous; with Yorkshire geniality and business acumen he must have been able to find quality tack at giveaway prices with all the racing and hunting stables empty. He only put a few shillings on for himself and for a few pounds I had saddle and bridle and head collar for Folly, as I called her.

During the summer I dragged an old tractor tyre round the farm with her, using Dolly's tack and then for seven pounds bought a Stanhope Gig, another of Harry's bargains, and a set of harness to put on her. I also bought the most beautiful reversed-hide side-saddle for five shillings and taught myself to ride on it, but never felt very safe jumping. In the early forties a few horse shows and gymkhanas were put on for the Red Cross and other charities. My lovely mare would go at a floating trot sometimes twelve or fifteen miles, and undressed into saddle and bridle would enter every class, winning many showjumping, handy horse and gymkhana events besides the driving classes which were very fully supported, as everyone was breaking their riding horses and hunters to harness. There were some very beautiful turn-outs in the driving classes for ancient Victorian vehicles had been dug out from under sheets at the back of coach houses where now surplus automobiles languished on blocks, under sheets, seeing the war out.

Folly, like every other privately owned horse, was denied access to any short feed, that is, bran, oats etc unless they were on essential work. So she was left unclipped and kept at grass. However, sadly, the ubiquitous Dolly was grounded for some months because of a low Ringbone diagnosis (I was never convinced of the accuracy of this because very few working farmers used top vets, whilst there were a few unqualified men, which would have been called farriers in previous times, who charged very little for their advice). No doubt her reckless and brook-no-restraint progress on the milk run contributed to her lameness, and it was at this point that the boss faced with empty milk float shafts, suggested I might like to use Folly in her place. She would then qualify for a handsome ration of corn, best hay and a stall in the Georgian nag stables. I was more than happy to oblige and was given an introduction by Syd to his bookmaker who he asked to help me. Cycling down to his racing yard now nearly closed down for the war, I found only a harness cob or two awaiting sale.

He took me to his tack room and opened two huge chests of rugs and said I could take what I wanted. It was a great thrill for a working girl who was kitting her first horse out, and I selected beautiful quality (unseen today) navy woollen day rug, and a red and black striped camel rug and a jute night rug and roller, for which I paid him the tiny sum he asked; my mare smelled of mothballs for the next three months.

After this I had to get round my unattached young boss — who was beginning to succumb to land girl charm — to get out the old hand-operated horse clippers and find some new blades (for Dolly was quite impossible to clip being extremely flighty, and on one occasion, only managed to submit to a patch the size of a newspaper on one side, before throwing in the towel). Folly was however perfectly amenable and not only did I have a lesson in clipping but he took on the considerable labour of turning the gearing handle to supply the power. No harness clip for me! She was to have a hunter full-clip and cherished with warm rugs and good corn, was to be the horse of my dreams.

Flying into Guildford after the milk run with loads of calves and sheep, my blond hair flowing behind me, I was nicknamed Boadicea — the yellow float, somewhat small for the mare, was repainted by my boss, and with the mare's coat shining like satin, I was regularly given a diva's reception by the farmers and stockmen from the pens. You may be sure the spotless striped camel rug was laid across her quarters whilst she waited at the pens!

At the age of seventeen I was called up into

the Land Army, and very slowly the cherished kit arrived. Green pullover and two Aertex shirts arrived fairly promptly but there were weeks of waiting for black lace boots. Khaki dungarees and khaki dust coat. Corduroy breeches were next and eventually a very smart heavy greatcoat with the WLA armband and a wide-brimmed felt hat. As clothes had been on ration for ages I had hitherto been wearing the most awful collection of the family's old pre-war cast-offs, by today's standards real refugee wear. Working with cows, the most important of all were wellies; these were last to arrive and were very short, with waterproof canvas tops, jolly comfortable actually as they were very light. Months later a really voluminous black fireman's type mac followed. This although heavy was completely waterproof and with a flared panel at the back, I could sit bareback on a wet day and by pulling this panel between my thighs, keep clean and dry even on a hot sweaty horse going down to the horse pond.

I was allowed to stay on at Manor farm and was regularly checked by the WLA local organiser and the many girls on local farms were invited occasionally to our organisers for tea. Most of us were pretty shy and engaged in stock farming because the arable girls were usually called up into gangs by the war Agricultural Committee and lived in hostels, being driven about in lorries, to wherever they were required. There were many Northern girls, and some out of London and from industrial towns; we all privately considered them rather fast! They worked in turbans with their hair underneath in curlers and went out to the pubs for their social life, in the evenings. In the summer they cut the legs off their dungarees into very daring shorts, and wore their hats at a very rakish angle.

I was lucky still to be billeted at home, but I was ambitious to improve my experience with dairy cows and attended night classes at the Guildford Tech in agricultural microbiology and dairy management with the Guildford Young Farmers' Club and so with considerable difficulty extricated myself from Manor Farm, my boss by this time having discovered a burning passion for me, with the local WLA organiser sympathetic to him. It being difficult to persuade the authorities to agree to let me fill a post on a machine-milked shorthorn herd on a farm a short distance away, milking forty cows with one other girl. Eventually in late spring I said my farewells to them although in fact I continued to keep in close contact with them all at Manor Farm.

Beryl and I had to share a bedroom in the foreman's cottage, which was semi-detached to the Carter's house next door. It was soon hot summer weather and I had to cycle four miles home to get a hot bath. Washing in the billet was confined to an enamel bowl in the kitchen, though we did have an outside loo. After a few weeks we began to scratch at angry looking lumps all over our bodies, our host's children as well. The itching started as soon as we got into bed. One night I had taken my big torch up with me (having just managed to get some batteries for it, which were all but unobtainable at that time). I called to Beryl and asked her if she was itching too — she was! So we both got up very quickly and flashing the torch, discovered bedbugs all over the sheets. When pursued with the torch they rushed at great speed into the corner of the room and into a huge crack in the skirting, leading to the next-door house.

This was too much! I believe they got the Council to sulphur-smoke both houses to kill the pests, which made me extremely unpopular with everyone! However as I was good with the cows and bull they wanted me to stay on, and although the other Land Army girl was found another place, I asked Ma for my old room back and cycled the four miles to work at four-thirty every morning. To get any lunch I rode my employer's lovely green young chestnut four-year old gelding home using the byways connecting the Portsmouth Road to Quarry Street, Guildford, which was Dolly's favourite spooking place, when the Army traffic was using it. This necessitated crossing the River Wey over the causeway next to the City Generating plant and now turned into the *Yvonne Arnaud Theatre*.

Arrived at home in the Great Quarry — a small collection of houses in this ancient quarry above the river, I would tie Paddy to the front gate — a substantial heavy oak job, whilst I ate ma's super lunch and then return to the farm, driving the cows up their fields nearer the gate for milking on the way up to the stables to unsaddle, Folly being once again relegated to the fields. Paddy benefited from this regular use and my new employer — married this time, no great horseman, felt decidedly safer when he rode him out. One day however the family gardener, arriving for an afternoon session on the borders informed us: 'That ginger horse has taken the front gate off the hinges and is half way down the hill!' Still in fact tethered to the gate and browsing over one of our neighbour's garden fence. Poor Ma and Pa! Anyhow he was recovered safe and sound and with a little adjustment to the hinges never did it again. The oak gate was a little heavier than Dolly's tethering block and had served the same purpose. Tying up horses in the old-fashioned stalls had taught the rudiments of good civilised behaviour; I tremble to think what would have been the result had he been one of today's boxed hunters.

5

The war was now getting pretty horrible. Food was short and most of the men were called up for national service. On this two hundred and fifty acre farm there was only Dave the Carter, now turned tractor driver, me and the Governor full time, and two octogenarians living in cottages at the buildings the other end of the farm. The Governor came into help milk from time to time, and helped with the bull when there were cows to serve; otherwise I was on my own. We milked with an Alfa-Laval two-bucket vacuum line plant in the cow stalls. I got all the cows' tails and udders and flanks clipped with the vacuum clippers, so it was easy to wash them before milking. We had a large number of home-reared heifers coming into the herd, so there were several to break in for the milking process, which I enjoyed, and the bull went out on a tether all day.

It was usual to have a weekend (after twelve on Saturday until Morning milking on Monday) off every three weeks. After so many early mornings I could never sleep in on my morning off without getting an appalling migraine, so I was always very short of sleep. However in the middle of a war you counted your blessings, and were lucky if your relatives in the services had avoided death or injury. My brother's school friends in the Navy were having a terrible time running the blockade and there were so many losses all round, you couldn't feel sorry for yourself.

In the spring when the cows were out at grass, I was told to get one of the carthorses in Thill harness (pad and crupper) and hitch onto a dung cart taking a spare horse in trace harness tied on behind, and go up to the secondary buildings when the dairy had been sterilised and the cowsheds washed and cleaned out. Here between milkings I had to get manure out of the ancient buildings with the help of the two octogenarians. The manure had accumulated from the inwintering of the home-reared heifers, over a couple of years and was piled up to the eves where the cattle had had to go mountaineering to lie on fresh straw on the top.

It was a satisfying job as day after day we attacked the steaming manure, loading it on the first dung cart which I would then lead out, the trace horse straining to help his mate in the shafts, because we were raking it out into small heaps at regular intervals on the side of the steep chalk slopes of the fields below the Hogs Back. Whilst I was away with the horses the two old chaps had propped up the shafts of a spare dung cart they kept at the buildings and were busy filling the next load up when I got back. Later of course, they would both go to the stacked heaps and spread the manure by hand — practised in putting a level dressing out to be ploughed in for the following crop.

Day after day we toiled between milkings; the two old chaps were very good-humoured, they and their wives lived in complete isolation so a new face was made very welcome. Their wives pressed morning tea and biscuits on me; like most country people they were curious to know how I spent any spare time, which was usually with young Farmers' Club activities, and were always dying to know if I had found Mr Right! They never really believed me when I said I did not want to find him before I was twenty-four, because I loved farm work and the idea of house-bound domesticity was appalling!

While I was at this farm my young boss became the victim of nervous depression and I had to work harder and harder with practically no help. Learning to drive the little grey Ford Ferguson tractor I was dispatched with a flat trailer filled with sulphate of ammonia in two-hundredweight bags to be unloaded at the second farm. This had gone absolutely solid the stuff having congealed completely. As the octogenarian was very weak on the other end of the stick we held to load and unload, it was killing work for an eighteen-year-old girl. The dog-fights in the skies above us were sometimes so severe that we often had to shelter under a trailer whilst pieces of aircraft drifted down. It was difficult work so that in late summer we felt that we were not far off the front line.

We had a really excellent Guildford vet and because the herd had a history of premature calvings he advised us to sign the herd on to the newly organised Ministry Veterinary Panel Scheme. This treated I seem to remember: contagious abortion with S19 vaccine, tuberculosis testing, mastitis and calf scours, the latter with the newly discovered sulphanilamide, the very first of the antibiotics, which had been found to be miraculous at the war front for treating the wounded. Dear Eric Barratt, what a marvellous vet he was! Having served in the First World War as an equine vet in the Horse Lines, he had a fund of fascinating reminiscences, a terrific sense of humour and a great enthusiasm for the new scheme which was to drag dairy husbandry out of the Stone Age. He spared no efforts to enlighten me of the very latest treatments and techniques, and as this herd had suffered periodic outbreaks of abortion with heifers slipping calves and being incarcerated subsequently in the isolation box which had never before been properly scrubbed or cobwebbed, my employer gave me a job which was dangerous in the extreme, without benefit of masks or proper disinfectants, as I brought down infected cobwebs and the dust of ages.

Within a few days I felt very ill indeed, and crawled home to bed with a raging fever, severe headache and aching limbs reducing erratically to subnormal temperatures and wicked shivering fits. When the doctor was called she recognised it immediately as undulant fever, the human equivalent of brucellosis from the Brucella abortis organism. Vets were in terror of getting a dose accidentally from a syringe full of vaccine, missing the target when large numbers of stroppy young bovines had to be caught up for routine vaccinations, the unfortunate human getting the dose instead. Of course with today's substantially made metal cattle-crush, the animals are held securely for treatment — it was different then.

Anyhow I was extremely ill with this unpleasant disease, and it was many weeks before the doctor would allow me to go back to work, so very thin and weak, I resigned my place with WLA agreement. I sold my lovely Folly to my best school friend who I knew would cherish her as I did (she in fact put her down at the ripe old age of twenty-seven) so that I could take up work as herd manager of a pedigree herd, if I could find it.

After such a baptism by fire as I had experienced in my last job, I was lucky to find just the niche in the cattle breeding world I wanted. This time with a family business where husband and wife were working hard to build up a dairy retail business from a small rented family farm. They had recently bought another farm two miles away, which was managed by a young Scot who was building up a pedigree Ayrshire herd for them. My responsibility was a small pedigree Guernsey herd, which was being up-graded by a recent purchase of well-bred Cornish heifers from George Blight's Tregonning herd. We had a first-class young bull of fashionable lines, which went out every day on a tether on the common next to the church yard; on one occasion he was found to have got off his chain and wandered in for a visit! The cow sheds were paved with black Victorian-type bricks, and there was a huge hayloft over (which was put to good use on VE Day celebrations). The herd was milk-recorded and hand-milked and some extra boxes which housed youngstock or surplus milkers had just been bought from Tom Mix's racing yard and I was told one of them had housed 'April Fifth' a successful racehorse winner.

As this was a Tuberculin-tested showing-herd none of the cattle were dishorned, as they would be now, and horns were carefully trained where necessary with a contraption of lead weights which were slipped over the horn tips of young animals, straps holding the horns in the right position rather like a dental brace. For shows and sales the horns were scraped with a piece of glass from a broken milk bottle and a beautiful shine put on them by polishing them with linseed oil. This together with rugging and discreet clipping of tail, udder and jowl, their golden well-washed coats, gleaming, clean white tails plumed out by washing and plaiting with straw made a real picture for the sale ring.

Although we had between twenty and thirty to handmilk, I had some help in the mornings from the boss after he had got off on the rounds three or four fairly decrepit milk vans driven by the female roundsmen. As we were in a frost pocket getting these started was liable to be a long laborious process of towing each to start in the depths of winter, while the boss's wife and one girl bottled up my milk as soon as it had gone through the cooler.

There was always a dicey period when all the water froze up, when I made sure that the cowshed was kept cosy, to keep the water bowls in front of the cows from freezing up completely. Coming in on a cold dark winter's morning to hand-milk was a much pleasanter occupation than operating today's draughty, chilly, milking parlours and with my mini radio tuned in to the Forces programme I had jolly old Glen Miller to keep me in touch with the latest dance music. Before afternoon milking, the cows' quarters clipped to show their silky udders, tails washed, golden straw beds and black bricks shining behind them with a pre-milking hose-down, it mirrored the model dairy as illustrated in the Victorian gentleman farmers' handbooks and I was not amused when visitors who came to see the cows milked, commented on how clean they kept themselves.

When every cow's yield is recorded twice a day, there is the added interest of relating the results of a new field of grass, or a different feeding stuff. All our feeds were hand-mixed and I remember *Scott Watson's Handbook*, the latest word on comparative food values at that time, was always to hand because we were never sure what concentrates would be available, as shipping was having a terrible time outrunning the German U-boats and we had to mix whatever was available from the feed merchant. Brewers Grains were a staple diet and these were stacked hot and steaming on arrival, under waterproof sacks on the concrete yard — shovelling the stuff into Bushel measures to put in the cows' mangers for afternoon milking. Of course the ubiquitous mangold was another staple, but silage was not generally made at that time. Decorticated cotton cake arrived in huge corrugated slabs, and had to be put through a curious type of hand-operated grinder to reduce it to crumbs. One winter we had to use barley straw as forage for the milking herd as hay was short.

At that time a thousand gallons average per cow in the herd, was what we were aiming for and this would average nearly five percent butterfat. As the weekly ration for humans was some two ounces of butter a week, the butterfat was urgently needed for our nutrition. At the age of eighteen, doing a long heavy day's work, I was always hungry as I shared a meagre school lunch with the pupils at the village school at midday, and though I was in a delightful billet with the retired parents of the boss's wife, I had only tea with them and then a candle to bed! After a while my boss came across me eating the cows' flaked maize, and noting my reducing weight got his wife to feed me breakfast and lunch, so as she was clever with the rations, I lived very well indeed.

As the milk round was getting larger all the time, a very nice milk pony was taken in with one of the rounds; this plus the ten-year-old son's riding pony was in my care, and for my use. Although quite small at under fourteen hands they were stocky and lively and I taught young Michael, the son of the family, to ride and used them for my enjoyment too.

In summer the milking herd went onto newly seeded leys just under the gibbet at Hindhead by day. This was a very long distance to drive the cattle to and fro for evening milking. They had to be driven cross-country, the track going through uncultivated commons, overgrown with bushes in which the cows would obstinately linger on hot days, trying to scratch the flies off their backs under the blackthorn bushes. This was when I made my first acquaintance with working dogs. Gareth, a well trained Border collie, resided on a chain by his kennel in the main yard, when not being taken round the farm by our boss, and was allowed to come with me and drive and collect the cows during their trek to the Hindhead foothills.

He was a wonderful dog and taught me so much. Between us, I riding one of our little ponies bareback — I simply unhooked one from their tethers on the common outside the buildings, and popped a bridle over the head collar so I could tie the pony up, if required by a really recalcitrant cow. The three-mile drive was a real pleasure and on arriving at the huge reseeded area I had to really use my voice to call the cows up from this wonderful grazing. One of the local farm workers told me afterwards, it was just like a hunting morning to hear me call up the cows! Gareth and I had to then shepherd them home slowly and carefully, making sure that they did not dally in the roughs and scratch their udders, I at the head of the herd, and the dog quietly keeping up all stragglers. Border collies are silent workers, unlike the Australian equivalent who open their mouths very wide. After that first summer I was a convert to the breed and have kept and bred them all my life.

6

My only chance of continuing the evening lectures at Guildford Tech. with my Young Farmers friends, was to cycle to Haslemere Station about a two mile ride and catch the Portsmouth-London train to Guildford. I then had a longish walk to get to the Tech. Occasionally I got a lift in one of the lad's cars with one or two others if the train arrived on time. Altogether by today's standards it was quite a hazardous journey, as there were no corridor-type carriages at that time, but only single carriages of four seats a side. They were full of soldiers from Liphook and Milford camps, and the trains were likely to stop in a tunnel if air attacks were imminent. As the lighting was constantly going off, sometimes the only lights in the carriages were the seven or more sometimes glowing cigarettes of my fellow travellers.

On the way home we had the French Canadians, a generally wild lot, and likely to be rather the worse for drink. Unlike many lads today the soldiers treated us land girls with great respect. I never had any fear at all on these journeys, we were all doing a vital job and provided they were not given a glad-eye by the females they never took advantage of the situation.

The Guildford Young Farmers took part in the County Federation of Young Farmers' Clubs Competitions at Clandon Park. I entered the horse-work competition and had to harness up heavy horses in pairs for field cultivations, rolling and harrowing and also drive a pair ploughing. Arthur's tuition at Manor farm had prepared me for the more usual jobs and thank heavens I was not asked to set out a ploughed field as I would not have been trusted with this job at Manor farm.

The dairy management competition required practical experience in machine and hand milking. Answering questions on calf rearing and production of clean milk, rationing and so on, I came home with two First prize cards for these having beaten the Club Chairman and some of the boy members in the process for which I was never forgiven! Later in life when I applied for the tenancy of a County Council smallholding, one of these boys was preferred to me — such was the injustice of that time when women were allowed to succeed in wartime when they were needed badly but after the war the young males hogged the few available rented farms and females had to marry if they were ever to take their place as employers!

About this time the war Ag. Executive decided they would run a Surrey Clean Milk Competition, which my boss entered me for. All our milk went through a metal strainer, direct into a churn in the cow shed, the woollen filter taking out extraneous cow hairs or specks; the churn was then wheeled round to the dairy for cooling and bottling. I seem to remember that there were three visits in all from the stewards, who watched your milking technique on one cow and the yield was strained through their own filter which was then taken with them and kept as a ghastly record of your practice.

Naturally I always scrubbed the milking stools — these a hygienic ten inches from the ground — every morning in hot Soda and these with the udder cloth and fore-milk cup which was used on every quarter to check that there were no mastitis flecks present before milking, were taken outside to stand in the sun to dry. I had bought myself some very nifty little white cotton bonnets which were starched up like hospital headwear and the 'Missus' supplied the usual white overalls, starched to miraculous whiteness to accompany this. It was very difficult to get a completely unspecked filter, as if a cow moved whilst milking a hair was likely to fall in! Anyhow we were delighted to get second place in the end.

Learning to lead cattle is very important in showing, as is teaching the calves and heifers in the first place. The boss's method of teaching both bovine and girl was to get an in-calf heifer penned up with the aid of Alex, his stockman, at the other farm, and then drive me down in his ancient Studebaker (even older versions were dotted about the fields of the two farms with prongs attached for sweeping loose, well-turned hay from the windrows up to the elevator under the stack). These, untouched for nine months of the year and green with verdigris, would leap into life when needed — a marvellous testimony to the USA manufacturers. He would hand me the heifer, sometimes with a calf at foot if it had caught Alex out, and watch me up the farm drive leaving me two miles to break her into traffic, which was light but with Milford Camp so near, heavy Army traffic was always a possibility so I was glad to get home safely.

Leading young bulls was even more necessary. We did not use a bull pole direct to the ring, but a chain fastened around the horns running straight down the frontal bone, and through the ring and into the hand. Guernsey bulls have good temperament, and were quite cooperative if they knew they were going out on the tether for good grass, or when flies and heat, or cold rain lashed them on the tether and their warm box and waiting tea gave them the required lively, jaunty gait. As we got more cows and the milk round got up to eight hundred gallons a day, we managed to get another girl to help me — this was rather essential as I was needed to take cattle up to the Reading Pedigree sales and also to show the young bull in his classes at Newbury, Cranleigh and Alton shows.

Towards the end of the war, much money changed hands at the sales of pedigree herds. The titled and wealthy who would in peace time be deeply involved in racing and hunting, had built up pedigree herds on their estates during the war and it became quite chic to arrive at the sale ring with super fitted picnic hampers (worth a bomb as collectables today) toted by their chauffeur or herds manager and immaculate wool tartan rugs to spread over the strictly utilitarian wooden step-seats of the auction ring. From this vantage point they either watched their herdsman in the ring with their entries or were a formidable force to be reckoned with, if you fancied the same lot number as they did.

Farming was a very *in* thing with the

well-heeled in society at that time. After VE Day bulls released from the German occupation of the Channel Isles made over 3,000 guineas on occasion, which allowing for inflation was a huge price by today's standards. Later on I was in a party of Guernsey breeders visiting the Island and viewing the lovely cattle which somehow the Islanders had managed to keep despite the occupation. The Island breeders were wonderful characters, but I was less enchanted by some of my well-heeled companions on the visit, who did not take too long to get out of farming after the cessation of hostilities.

I, like the other herdsmen, knew the big spenders and this stood me in good stead when I was later appointed to buy and sell cattle myself. For the time being I learned my trade and took over the pedigree bookwork in the farm office after work at night. Stock registrations and six generation pedigree of animals going for sale, milk records ready for the Milk Marketing Board milk recorders who visited regularly to check our figures. Veterinary records on all animals treated and with what drugs.

Witley Park, a very large estate close by, had at that time two top quality herds of Guernseys and Ayrshires the latter of which seemed to have monumental difficulties with stockmen. The farm manager who had bought some top quality Scottish-bred Ayrshires, sent his pedigree registrations and a set of herd books for me to collate and the names of the Bargower Miss Donald's which went into umpteen generations were stamped indelibly into my memory for life.

The day came when Witley Park asked my boss if I could be spared to take six heifers up to the Ayrshire Society sales at Reading. I was rather chuffed about this until the animals were unloaded at Reading for me in the most awful state: unclipped (a big thing with Ayrshires who had to have the head and neck completely clipped out), untrimmed and absolutely filthy! With a day or two to spare I had a terrific session with the hose and got them all snow-white, then when dry, their heads tails and udders clipped, horns scraped and oiled and a neat job of topiary with scissors to get the top-line absolutely straight. Unlike Guernseys all the hair of the coat had to be lightly damped and the hair brushed against the normal lie of the coat whilst still damp, to make the bodies as square as possible. Pedigree stockmen were usually the most good natured lot you could find anywhere, and with two really stroppy individuals, I could rely on one of the other early arrivals to give me a hand, as I did them.

My boss and the Witley Park manager together with one or two other local farming families, were great bridge and whist players, and at one of these family functions it was decided that they would try and find me a decent horse. Jake, a local dealer, had a nice four-year-old filly, an unbroken three-quarter thoroughbred, by Tidal Wave for sale and I went up to his yard at Hindhead to see her. She was about sixteen hands and dark brown (for some reason horses are rarely called black which is what she looked like to me). I fell for her immediately, and paid a very reasonable price for her, and called her Minerva.

Of course I was extremely busy with the cattle so finding time to ride — leave alone break a young horse was difficult. Minnie was difficult to catch even when turned out with the friendly ponies, and putting her into breaking harness (circingle and long reins) was impossible on my own and my fellow herds-girl rather disinclined to help as she had a serious boy friend.

After a week Jake, my dealer friend, called in at the farm very concerned, to tell me that he would send a groom down to help me if I was having trouble. I gathered he had heard someone had broken a leg trying to back her (shades of my early relationship with Dolly) my good friends in the farming community, cautioning him about selling me a dangerous young horse.

By the time I was in the next stage of breaking and ready to back her, the clocks had gone back, the fields were incredibly wet and her two pony friends had been moved elsewhere. I had to see her after work in the dark (the boss called in on the early morning outdoor stock rounds). To my dismay the poor mare went desperately lame due to a foot abscess, which the farrier excavated. Trudging across wet fields in pitch black, armed with a hurricane lamp, a bucket, boiling water, Kaolin poultice, sack bandages (no spare First Aid bandages in wartime) Minnie would see my lamp and hear my sploshing progress, neighing a ringing welcome. Tying her to the gate post, I dressed her foot carefully and made a great fuss of her in her solitude, giving her a short feed of cow-mix as she was running some pretty rough ground though with plenty of grass. The foot took quite a long time to heal, with the farrier having several goes with his knife to get the pus out of every cranny.

Every cloud has a silver lining as the saying goes, and the result of this unfortunate lameness and my efforts to treat her, was that

Minnie became my loving slave, and by the time she had recovered I was able to get her nearer the buildings in a little paddock with a big beech tree next to the gate. We then had a month of brilliant moonlit frosty nights resulting in some heavy enemy air raids. After work I got a saddle on her on my own, and mounted her via the gate (I was never any good at vaulting!)

After a few days she decided to lead me a dance starting to move off bucking as I climbed on. Having been dropped painfully a couple of times, it was back to the drawing board. I consulted my Victorian reference book in horse-breaking, and purloining a large wagon rope, put a running noose round her girth, the loose end passing through a rope neck strap and under the jaw strap of a good old fashioned cart-horse head collar; this was then tied to the tree with a quick release knot. According to my directions, you were then ready to show the young horse any alarming object — such as putting up an umbrella or indeed any object that had caused alarm before. I got someone to leg me up into the saddle, but without stirrups, the mare shot back and felt the noose tighten round her girth, and jumped forward with a gasp! That was the last time she even moved a hair whilst I was mounting, although for another three weeks I left a coil of rope loose on her withers whilst I mounted.

Of course any experienced person would consider the risks of breaking single-handed in the moonlight totally unacceptable. Fortunately for me someone upstairs watched over us and Minnie made a really lovely riding horse. On my days off I arranged to hack her to the nearest meets of the Chiddingfold Farmers Foxhounds, a pack which had been formed in wartime using borrowed country, to try and keep down the plague of foxes which had multiplied in the dearth of hunting since the outbreak of war. The nearest meets were seven or eight miles, and in the very limited fields of followers at that time, she gave me some wonderful days, with long hacks home in the twilight. Service men and women in wartime hunted for free so I wore my WLA uniform with a soft hat. Minnie had to live out but half-clipped under a New Zealand rug. With long slow walking to and from hunting she became super-fit.

Today, when we are bombarded with American hype on 'bonding' and advance-and-retreat techniques in animal training, I remember my lovely teenage horses, every one of which would follow me everywhere without use of the reins, even in a dense crowd. Friends use to roar with laughter when I pretended to hide from Minnie, having dismounted and left her with the reins secured under the stirrup leathers. Quietly at a walk she would carefully pick her way through a crowd, until she caught up with me again.

7

By 1945 we were all heartily sick of the war. Even my exuberant teenage temperament began to be affected by the constant shortages of food and clothes and petrol. If the doodlebugs were downright frightening, the ominous quiet coming after the cessation of the peculiar throbbing noise of their motivation, followed by an explosion that would make anyone but a zombie jump, the rocket phase which followed this German invention was even worse, the high-pitched screaming as it soared over you, and the ultimate crash even if it did not land near this time, convinced you it was unlikely you would escape much longer. The damage in the towns was awful, but as they were lobbed over in a very indiscriminate way, living away from the centre of a military target or a large town did not make much difference and we all felt very nervy and jittery.

My brother was serving in North Africa, my brother-in-law in Malaya. They miraculously escaped casualty or capture. Pa was in the Home Guard as was my boss, my mother a Red Cross volunteer, and my sister, now pregnant, was still fire-watching at nights. When eventually the second invasion commenced we were very excited and apprehensive. Unlike today when a war is conducted against a constant babble of info coming from 'The Box', we were not used to getting much news at all 'Be like Dad — keep Mum!' the posters adjured us. I remembered seeing the strange looking concrete rafts anchored in the Helford River in Cornwall when I had a week's leave with a friend at the *Budock Vean Hotel* in early autumn (subbed by pa). It was all very hush hush, and now it seemed that these had joined with hundreds of others, manufactured and hidden in West Country estuaries and anchorages and were on their way to the French coast, as invasion barges to carry the troops right onto the beaches.

We remembered all too well the disastrous first invasion, when our troops were driven remorselessly back to Dunkirk and the fragments of our Army were rescued by a fleet of little fishing and pleasure-boats the owners of which bravely risked their lives to bring our soldiers home. Therefore of course the subsequent savage fighting over many fronts, the sketchy news and finally the fantastic reports that the Allies in Europe had won the war, lifted our spirits incredibly, even though fighting was still going on in the eastern theatre. VE Day will never be forgotten by our generation. Even in the quiet countryside we needed no mass celebrations to savour the moment.

It was agreed that we would stage a VE Party in the hayloft over the cowsheds. With all the roundsmen needed for the retail business, the second farm staff, and all our neighbouring farmers and milk customers we were a jubilant crowd. I and Mary got a tractor driver and flat-trailer, and picked fresh beech sprays in green and copper to decorate the roof joists joining to the floor to make attractive bowers. The village electrician found a mass of coloured lights. The Missus got her sisters in to make pastries and somehow beer and spirits were purloined. The electrician, who also organised the local dances for the military, came up with recording equipment, and everyone in the village who knew the family, turned up with chairs.

It was decided that we would all wear fancy dress, and so my sister rooted out a Scandinavian outfit for me. The boss affected a Thomas Hardy type of outfit and the Missus, her old Girl Guide uniform; others were ingeniously made out of the limited wardrobes of the time. The barn looked absolutely lovely and the atmosphere was wonderful. The cows were milked early, their yields down appallingly — clearly disliking the disturbing noises coming from the ceiling. We had to get to the party by ladder, as there were no steps up. After a wonderful party some of the biggest celebrants had to be watched down carefully! It was the first real party I had ever enjoyed and quite unforgettable by all present.

Getting the cows milked next morning, and the delivery vans away on time was another story, but who cared! Only those whose loved ones were still fighting the enemy in the East had some reservations but it was felt that peace there must soon be on the way. The large majority had some very real cause for celebration. I was asked at this time by a Young Farmers' Club boyfriend to come to his twenty-first birthday party — it was to be a very posh affair with dinner jackets and long dresses for the girls, a change after the war shabbiness. I was contemplating acceptance, when word reached me (the jungle drums of farming society!) that his family were expecting an engagement announcement. Whether this was correct or complete invention, it was quite sufficient to make me send a 'Regrets' card, which caused a certain amount of disappointment the other end and scotched any rumours of this sort. I intended no lifelong commitment at this time, although I felt that I would like to get further up the farming ladder, and to this effect, I kept my eye on the Sits Vacant in the *Farmer & Stockbreeder* until I saw a place for a herd manager to build up a pedigree herd for a new owner.

The farm was in Berkshire, not too far from Reading, and when I drove (in pa's old Alvis Coupe) over to my interview, I must say the countryside seemed very flat and cold after the cosy Surrey Hills. However viewing the setup, which included fertile fields, good yard and a new milking parlour and some excellent boxes, I succumbed to the prospect of buying in pedigree Guernseys for an absent owner, who was something in the City and resided in a beautifully refurbished manor house. The billet was not so good though — an extremely cheerless unheated bothy in the yard, and meals either with Nanny in the Big House, or with the general handyman and his wife. I think I made a great mistake when I chose the latter — but anyhow I moved in and worked out the sterilisation routine for the parlour and bought in over the next few months, some very useful first-calf heifers which I taught to go through the bale fairly efficiently and also a nice young bull to run with them. In the autumn it was depressingly foggy and chilly on the Berkshire 'flats' and the parlour was absolutely freezing despite the handyman's efforts with a blow-heater!

The cows managed to bring in a lot of mud with them, so there was a lot of cleaning off to do, before getting the clusters on for milking. The handyman's wife was an atrocious cook and we existed on some very dreary spam-type meals, with the use of a very cold bathroom. After work the evenings seemed very long on my own, with only a radio for company, but I kept occupied with the cow records, we were daily recording, and managed to setup my employer with a very decent little herd in the next few months.

I shall never know whether it was the spam (a particularly flaccid wartime meat substitute) or something else which struck me down with the most appalling dysentery and sickness and symptoms of food poisoning. I carried on as long as I could, but the pervading cold and damp of my lodgings did not help matters, and the boss had to get in a replacement milker whist I tottered home to ma to recover.

This was another fairly long convalescence, during which time my parents convinced me that if the living conditions were so bad, I would probably go down again with the same trouble in due course — so very sadly I had to tender my notice to a very kind and understanding employer. My lovely Minnie having been sold to a local lady at Hindhead before I left the area — I was fancy-free and without equine impediment — which was as well as few employers relish having an employee's horse thrust upon them — and moreover would be likely to offset the wages considerably if they did take one on.

My next job was nearer home in the Surrey Hills, where some newcomers to farming were setting up a pedigree Jersey herd. Their little estate of 30 acres was very attractive, they were very accomplished property improvers, skills which I was interested to learn, and had converted some barns into a really lovely home. There was a little cowshed close to the back door and they already had six cows and a milking machine. It was incredibly cold in winter 1946/7 but I was able to milk the cows in their stalls using plenty of straw for bedding, then as I was living en-famille, come into the luxury of an Aga-heated kitchen and warm centrally-heated house. There was a girl already in residence in the 'maids' room' so I was given their really luxury guestroom which you can bet I kept in pristine condition so that when she found another job, I was allowed to remain there and not have to endure her room, which stunk of nicotine and cheap scent.

I was introduced to the breeding lines of the charming little Jersey cows and we got about looking at some very nice herds. Their teenage daughter, Dorothy had just left finishing school and I accompanied her on one or two train trips to London where the Ballet Russe, in wartime exile performed *The Firebird, Petrouchka* and the fiery Russian ballets which were my particular favourites. We also saw Puccini's *Bohemians*, I remember. There were very few taxis in London at that time, so you had to leg it to the tube to get home, although we were met by her parents at the station. Dorothy had a hunter up in the stables, which I was happy to exercise and do-up for her if she was going out.

The little Jersey cows were wonderful milkers, and we got the herd up to fourteen and cast around for a prolific bull, to knit them into a first-class herd. It was at this point that I remembered my old friend Syd's advice — 'Now then, my Gel,' he said. 'You just remember that it's very easy to be diddled when buying livestock. It isn't the hard-up little 'coper that will do you the dirtiest deal, for he has got to keep his reputation to find his next meal. Just you watch the gentlemen for some of them be proper bastards when it comes to palming off disasters!'

Unfortunately the buying of the bull was not left in my hands. Mrs Caruthers, Dorothy's mum, rather fancied socialising with London society women, and was at that time very friendly with a titled lady who had an excellent high-yielding herd of Jerseys, quite close to us. She had decided to sell her six-year-old bull which when we went to have a look at him was domiciled in a bull-pen which had every type of constraint in it, including an overhead pulley for the bull to be chained if necessary, and, ominously, quick release slits in the pen walls for attendants to get out in a hurry. The herdsman gave me an unfathomable look, and said he took the bull out every day to go on a tether, but always used a bull-pole which wasn't surprising on a senior bull.

Many tricky Jersey bulls are led out with two attendants, one on each side, so that he is unable to get at the leader with his horns. Jersey females are docile and kind, males are a different proposition. We inspected some nice quality daughters of this bull which were milking like mad. Mrs Caruthers fell for a special price for this 'Marvellous foundation sire for you, Mary dear' and he was sent over for me to look after. At the time we only had some largish wooden cattle boxes. I usually caught up the bull with a feed bucket in my hand, for serving cows or going out to daily exercise on the tether.

At this time there were large numbers of Italian and German prisoners of war working on the land, and Kurt, one of these, was dropped every morning, and collected at night by one of the war Ag: lorries. Hans employed just down the road was a sunny tempered Bavarian who had a penchant for thatching, and remained in this country after the war. Kurt's knowledge of English was quite good, but he was smouldering with hate, since his family in Dusseldorf had had a really terrible time in the allied bombing offensive. They were all close to starving, and I guessed his sister had had to turn to 'the oldest profession' to get enough food for the family. It was therefore unfortunate for me that as Kurt was mucking out the cow sheds, and I was across the yard at the bull box, the moment I put the bull on the pole, in a second he ducked his head, and managed to break the wooden bull pole on his horn, in contact with the walls of his box.

Of course after the war bull poles were made of metal and unbreakable. A horned bull with a grievance and a bleeding nose on which three inches of stick dangled was very dangerous indeed. I called Kurt again and again as I was unable to get out as the door was on the wrong side of the bull, but he was being difficult and would not come. I was by then in the corner the bull's nose on the ground well out of my reach. All I could do was by gripping the horns keep them on either side of my body whilst I called and called to Kurt. Thank God, he eventually sauntered in with sullen features, which changed immediately he saw my plight. With a four-tined fork in his hand he managed to distract him long enough for me to slip through the door, and bar it up again. This episode made me very weak at the knees, and when the vet came to treat a mastitis case next day, he told me this bull had had a go at his former herdsman — which is probably why they had decided to sell it!

Mrs Caruthers had something to say to her Ladyship — but not too nasty, or the social life would suffer! He went back to their place and was eventually put down. I never heard of Guernsey, or South Devon bulls which we had in later years, ever being vicious but Jerseys can be little stinkers, and we knew of one who was always delivered to the new field on the farm by tying him to the back of a tractor trailer — the farmer's son being safely on top of the trailer. Anyhow after this episode we found a very nice young bull (a beautiful Mulberry colour) and he learned good manners right from the start and never tried to be naughty.

About this time Dorothy was offered the most beautiful horse I had ever seen. He was called Essex and had been the huntsman's horse of one of the Essex packs of foxhounds. He was a middle-weight of seventeen hands, and getting the rugs on him was quite a stretch. Perfectly mannered in every way, we got him fit, and I had some wonderful rides in the woods and over the commons of Winterfold. Dorothy however was rather nervous of him, and really preferred her 15.2 hand mare, so I was delighted to have the ride on him.

On Easter Monday, Charlie White used to put up a really nice course of hunter trial jumps at his Burwood Farm, near Guildford. Here the newly formed Chiddingfold Farmers' Foxhounds would parade and a host of competitors and well-wishers would turn up at this attractive site, in this lightly undulating plateau on the North Downs above Merrow. Here I had the ride of my life; never having competed in this type of event before, I was foolish enough not to walk the course, in fact

I had no one present to hold Essex, having hacked him over and did not want to leave him tied to a wagon rope against a hedge, as many of the other competitors did. With supreme confidence in my lovely safe mount, I entered the senior event, but never having met a drop-jump out hunting, was extremely surprised when what appeared to be a level course, included a nice little drop landing. To me it felt just like falling downstairs in a dream, but dear Essex carefully threw his head up, and put me back in the saddle and we got round fine!

The Guildford Young Farmers had a good summer programme, one evening of which was a cricket match at Rex Marshall's farm on the Loseley Park Estate. Rex was a father figure to the club at the time, training ex-soldiers up to agricultural workers ready for their demobilisation from the Services. On a fine summer evening after work, I hacked Essex over from Hascombe and joined them — in spirit — not at all sorry to be excused combat because of my horse. I never could get to grips with cricket! Among the young players was a very tall chap who had been invalided out of a tank regiment, who was doing his post-service training with Rex. I gave little thought at the time that my future was to be linked to his.

8

My employers decided to move out of their little holding — they had a very tempting offer I believe, and take a hundred and twenty acre farm on Blackdown Hill, near Haslemere, just under the beauty spot Temple of the Winds, with its wonderful views across West Sussex. The farm was down to good, though rather thin young three-year leys, and was watered by springs coming out from the hill and gathered into lakes on the farm. It was a very pretty place with its ancient farmhouse, flag-stoned floors and inglenook fireplaces. The yard was just below house level with a rectangle of tiled barns and boxes. There were two cottages and I was promised one of my own or a converted bothy.

Moving dairy herds to new premises is never easy as morning milking is done and milk sent off to the dairies, before bundling the poor old dears into lorries for their journey, and off-loading them again into a strange yard for the evening milking, all very unsettling for them and bad for the milk yields. Fodder, hand tools, cow cake, dairy equipment, the latter sterilised, has all to be in place for their arrival — a long way after their comfort comes the dogs, cats and finally their weary attendants who have probably been manhandling props such as wheelbarrows, corn and cake bins, hand tools and sacks of feed and a nefarious selection of farm clutter since daybreak, with great prominence being given to the veterinary cupboard for the cows, and very little thought being given to the whereabouts of the aspirin for the workers.

It was decided that I and my assistant, Kate would go ahead with Mr Caruthers with the livestock, and Dorothy and her mother would see to handing over the house to the new owners. No one had given much thought for the kitchen provisions, or comfort for the vanguard, so with the boss going back to supervise the furniture's progress the following day, we two girls put two mattresses down on the flagstones of the old kitchen, which had not had a fire lit for many a long day. Although it was midsummer I have never forgotten how the cold crept into my bones that first night. My hips ached for months — warning me of early arthritis — I am sure the result of sleeping on a damp floor after Herculean exercise during the move.

Gradually we got settled into the new

place. The cattle milked well and the riding over Blackdown was superb. It was a very beautiful place but getting to my evening lectures at Guildford Tech. was more difficult than ever, as the farm lane off the Haslemere to Midhurst road was very rough and isolated to return to late at night, particularly in the winter when completely dark, with only the dimly lit windows of two other properties on the way home to give a glimmer of light. My moped was never entirely reliable and was likely to be jettisoned as the road got steeper to be recovered by my employer next day.

After a while I decided to give the very highest yielders more chance to develop their full potential. Just three or four cows were allowed to lie in a loose box of their own at night, these few being milked three times a day, which meant the last milking was very late at night. However the spring water was very short of calcium and other minerals, so it was difficult to get enough calcium and magnesium into them, to prevent milk fever so I always had a flutter valve and needle and bottles of calcium Borogluconate and magnesium to hand to give subcutaneous injections if necessary. We bought some very well-bred but hard-done heifers from a herd dispersal and I asked if I could buy one for myself and pay for its keep out of my wages each week, as I had advised my employers that these were a really good investment.

Naturally the Caruthers' talents as property improvers were given full rein in this most interesting old property, so there was always a truck-load of builders at work. Mrs Caruthers bred show-quality standard poodles (these were surprisingly, to me, sporting and intelligent little dogs, if one overlooked their absurd topiary). For some reason these home-bred puppies were always suckled by Border collie bitches, all but one of their own litter being destroyed at birth — the remaining puppy allowed to suckle alongside the intruders. I fell in love with a little bitch: merle coloured (grey and white speckled with black) with one blue eye. I was furious because the stupid builders would keep pushing the puppy onto her back, and tickling her as if she was a fat Labrador. This treatment is liable to make a sensitive collie hate men for ever. I was delighted to be given Bonnie, as I called her, and she became my dear friend.

After some time at this farm I felt the need for a change. Living in with your employers, however charming, is something of a strain and my long-awaited cottage had failed to materialise, having now been rented to a relative of the family. At twenty-three with the men returning from the war, I realised that I was becoming so isolated that I might as well be in a religious order, and I had better get out and do something about it if I ever hoped to have a home of my own. I spoke to my employers in these terms, who tried to dissuade me — but in due course they managed to find a young man just out of agricultural college (who then married Kate!) and I arranged to sell my heifer at the Jersey Cattle Society's March sale at Reading, and then move on, living with my parents for a while, to try and make up for the hard-working war years, as ma and pa were on their own now. My brother-in-law was home from the war and my sister and he installed together with their three little girls.

Fortunately my heifer did very well at the sales, and having cost me originally forty pounds, made me two hundred and forty guineas, her keep having been docked from my wages each week. I decided that this being my first spring, solvent and fancy-free I would buy myself a demi-trousseau on this windfall, and then trip the light fantastic with my Young Farmers' Club and Young Conservative friends. Selling my heifer in the late morning, I changed and cleaned up as adequately as the very grubby market loos allowed, and then set off into the upmarket centre of Reading where I spent all afternoon buying an accordion-pleated, short-jacketed grey suit, a very luxurious by postwar standards summer coat, with sombrero buttons, two pretty summer dresses, and some light shoes. Then clutching my many expensively wrapped parcels, I caught the train back to Guildford and bussed the two miles home, to start a life of leisure, my little bitch Bonnie having proceeded me a few days before.

After living in digs all the war years my parents' home seemed absolute luxury. Whilst I had been away pa's health had become rather precarious; gassed in the First World War, he later had a long spell in the TB Sanatorium at Mundsley on the East coast which he found incredibly cold and cheerless but from which he made a marvellous recovery. He was in fact able to go on writing until the end of his life. Ma had given up her wartime chicken keeping and also relinquished daily help and some of her more arduous gardening activities. Food like most things, was still very short. I was able to take my little bitch out for good long training walks and borrow the family car to go and see my old friends at Manor farm.

It was not long before my friend, Jim Graham, the Estate Manager at Witley Park, rang me up to ask me if I would like a 'bargain'. This turned out to be an elderly pedigree Guernsey of impeccable lineage which had had 'summer mastitis' resulting in her losing two quarters in her udder. She was in-calf to a very valuable bull. Although a milking machine cluster could manage to stay on a three quartered cow, or even occasionally a two quartered cow on the diagonal, however two quarters gone on one side was totally impossible, and an unviable machine milker of this ilk would have only one future — at the abattoir, unless an unwary Guernsey enthusiast would take her on at her killing value.

Naturally he was a good psychologist and knew my weaknesses. I agreed to have her provided I could find some grass for her. Eventually I persuaded a Guildford grazier who rented the Shalfort meadows beside the River Wey and adjacent to my home, to let me have a small paddock adjoining, which he allowed the cricket club to rent for their Saturday matches, and Jeannette wearing a leather cow collar was ensconced there quite happily on her own, next to the beef stores, and was milked by me once a day when I hitched her to a tree, and carried the bucket and mini-churn home on my moped. Ma and I made a dairy out of a converted coal cellar and I supplied the family with milk, scalded cream and butter, Bonnie and the cat doing well on the skimmed milk.

9

At Easter Bonnie and I went up to Burwood hunter trials and once again met the tall ex-soldier I had met once before at the cricket match. There too I met some of my old YFC pals who reminded me that the Club's annual dance was in a week's time and to make sure not to forget the date. It was there as I stood doing a wallflower act amongst those hoping for partners, that I 'looked across a crowded room' as the song goes and saw that tall head dancing with my vivacious and pretty friend, Tessa, and sure enough I knew there and then that he was my Mr Right, and I must never 'let him go' as the song advises. All is fair in love and war so with all the guile, patience, wit and resolve I could muster, I quite shamelessly set out to know him better and if possible captivate him.

Fortunately for me, and I hope for him, we were mutually attracted to one another and in the month of June at a barn dance within a moonlit rose garden, Alan popped the question. By this time I was perversely having severe misgivings about losing my freedom and took a week to consider his offer of marriage, then we mutually agreed to have a year's engagement, hoping meanwhile to find some little farm of our own somehow.

Meanwhile with the incredible good luck that some beginners have, dear Jeannette turned out to be safely in calf, and as I had to dry her off prior to calving, I found another Guernsey ex-house cow to help the milk supply. Goblin was a very heavy milker and had to be milked twice a day.

The cricket club put up a little marquee to keep their clothes and other valuables in for a match day, and for some weeks nobly put up with cow pats in inconvenient places. However when the cows got into their tent one day, their forbearance was tested to the limit and my landlord very kindly explained their predicament and asked me to find the cows another home. Whilst I was looking for this with considerable difficulty, Jeanette calved a perfectly beautiful show quality heifer calf. A bull would have been acceptable because of its breeding potential, but a heifer was fantastic!

Swiftly cow and calf were entered in the September Guernsey Society's sale at Reading where the heifer made top price and dear old Jeanette would have at least another six months as a suckler cow, or might even be given another chance to breed. Both cows were moved to a little paddock under St Martha's church meanwhile, close to Halfpenny Lane. Here milking was much more difficult as I had a three and a half mile ride on unmade lane through the Chantries some of it deep with sand. The moped and its heavy mini-churn on the back made very heavy weather indeed of this. As I was a complete dead loss as a mechanic, it was frequently abandoned on the roads and tracks, for poor Alan who was by then a flourishing corn buyer, to recover and repair!

I was offered a little smallholding by a local Estate but only on a twelve months agreed term. We hoped that it might be possible to extend this in due course as the place was without any water or power and the cottage nearly derelict so it was unlikely to tempt anyone else. I got some nine Guernseys together and a piebald cob we called Sam and found in the Podgers yard. I managed to buy Dolly's old milk float from Manor farm as they had by then other transport. Sam was needed to get the milk churns down our derelict drive to the main road to be picked up by the milk lorry. After leaving the churns on another farmer's stand, I picked up our empty churns and took them into the estate's industrial site a short distance up the road and filled them with clean water for house and dairy use. The cows had a main supply trough in the front field, which being on sand did not get poached in wet weather.

Sam was a sweet horse and was also used in Folly's old gig at the weekends when Alan and I had some wonderful picnics with him, and I also used him for giving riding lessons so he had a large appreciative fan club, including our grey semi Persian cat, Sylvester, who adored him and after his nightly hunt in the old wooden cowsheds where we would sometimes find as many as two or three rat tails, the bales flung about all over the place, would retire to his comfortable perch on Sam's back, looking very smug.

I used oil lamps for lighting and a double-burner oil stove for cooking, which was efficient actually, using flat irons on a metal grid on top of the burners for ironing. There was a good copper for washing the dairy utensils and the clothes, and I had an old-fashioned kitchen range, which would just about boil a kettle and I could make toast on, so I, Bonnie and Sylvester had home comforts even in these spartan surroundings. Alan and I would sit in the evenings planning our future, before he had to get his motor bike started and get home before curfew

— eleven o'clock — our parents were very strict!

We were married the following spring, the reception being at my home, the wedding, in preference to my in-laws wishes, held at Shalford church, but we decided to keep the ceremony simple and without fuss, with nobody present but my two eldest nieces who did not want to miss the occasion! And our best man. All our friends came and we had no rain to make the garden reception tricky — there were few marquees in use at that time. The weather started with an incredibly early spring in 1949 and the summer was glorious and so dry that the grass was burned as brown as in the extreme drought of 1976.

The course of true love never did run smooth; a relative of the landlord required our farm after a short tenancy, and my parents took us in, the cattle and my lovely Sam having to go to a new home. A very sad time for me, but at least we had each other.

We started what was to be a lifetime interest in property restoration by buying our first small cottage — semi-detached in the middle of Shalford for six hundred pounds. In due course after Alan had dug and delved we found a Georgian fireplace behind the hideous Victorian arch. Upstairs we bared the beams in this modest little Georgian terrace cottage. In the forty's fashion we put a bath with a removable top in the kitchen and installed a Rayburn cooker. By this time we felt that we had developed the property as far as was prudent (a point we have always born in mind in subsequent renovations) and selling, as we fondly believed for £2,000. We bought a sixty-acre North Devon farm, with a completely renovated farmhouse with three bedrooms, a shippon for twelve cows, a large barn and a two-unit milking machine for this figure.

Brendon Farm, Holsworthy, North Devon,
1950–55. Our home-bred heifer.

Showing the bull

Bringing home the last of the hay crop

10

So it was that one early January I found myself clutching my baby son of five months on the Exeter-Okehampton train, Alan having gone on ahead with our furniture and a newly acquired ex-army pick-up, two days before to get the house, which had been empty for twelve months, ready for us. At that time it was possible to take the train right through to Bude, which passed through Holsworthy, our destination. As the train after Exeter turned into a very slow line, stopping at every Halt and companionably waiting for 'regulars' to arrive, usually accompanied by baskets of provisions and often small livestock such as dogs, goats and poultry.

Alan thought it would be better to pick us up from Okehampton, and I must say after a long journey I was very glad to get off the train. As I nursed Philip on my lap in the very chilly, draughty cab of our truck — an ex-army Ford V8 and very fuel-thirsty — the snow drifting against the windscreen I stared with interest at the Dartmoor Tors all gleaming white on the horizon, and listened to the horrors Alan had found on his arrival.

Apparently a plague of rats were occupying the walls of our cob-walled cottage. Scampering along the rafters under the floorboards upstairs. The previous owners had left a ton of corn in the adjacent barn after their hasty exit due to marital problems. The rats in the intervening time had lost no time in redistributing it around the floorboards and walls of the house for their convenience. (These we started battle with immediately, with rat poison, and eventually put our little white cat up in the loft, to enjoy the hunting, from which she refused to emerge for two months, having to be fed up there in the meanwhile.)

Alan was so put off by the noise of heavy bodies crashing around that when he found a dead owl in the Rayburn flue, he chickened out and drove into the *White Hart* in Holsworthy for the night. Later we found that the previous occupants had failed to recognise the rat noises and summoned a Churchman to exorcise the house of ghosts!

The semi-rotary pump at the sink from our well was very rusty having been idle so long, though in fact during the four years we were in residence it only produced discoloured reddish water. All the napkins were hung on the washing line, this disgusting colour, to be recovered after two hours or so bleached white as snow from the blustering Atlantic winds, for we were only a few miles from the wild coastline between Bude and Hartland Point.

My first impressions of the house when we arrived in our tiny hamlet were mixed because by then it was quite dark. It was semi-detached to another substantial house, backing onto the farmyard of the biggest farmer in the group. We had to light the three oil lamps on the kitchen table, before I could see what we had bought. Trustfully I had left Alan to buy our farm unaided by me but with the support of his brother, when a decision had to be made in a hurry. It was infuriating to me that because of heavy snow after our arrival, I did not see the grass fields for several weeks, but with the Rayburn going and a nice little log fire in the sitting room the two-foot thick walls kept us very cosy at this cold season, and like all traditional cob cottages lovely and cool in summer too.

The previous owners had decorated all the walls in cherry blossom pink with white paint on doors and woodwork including the enormous deep window sills which I kept decorated with huge bunches of wild flowers and berries, from early February until December. Our little paddocks being thick with wild snowdrops, daffodils and primroses and the high road banks down to our away fields, holding an inexhaustible supply of foxgloves, campion, stitchwort, may and honeysuckle all with lovely perfume and so much prettier than cultivated flowers.

Brendon farm not only had a modern bathroom, built into the adjacent barn, but also sensibly took all the rain water from the roof, into a tank for the cold water taps and toilet flushing, an idea which I would have thought by now would be obligatory in the building of today's housing estates in rapidly dwindling town-water supplies. When you depend on a well-water supply within a short distance of open cattle yards, it is sensible not to drink unboiled water, and a local doctor who was born in Australia, always preferred the locals to drink rainwater where possible. There was always a considerable demand for mineral water from the local store two miles up the road.

One of the luxuries our predecessor had thrown in was a small generator which could just modestly light house and barn, but as the shippon was a distance away we had to use a tilley storm lantern up there.

One of our difficulties was that the purchasers of our Surrey cottage had at the last moment of completion, failed to come up with the whole of the agreed purchase money.

This is such a regular dirty trick of purchasers that never since have I ever felt comfortable about arranging sale and purchase on the same day. Many years ago we should in this country have changed to the Scottish system, which guarantees a sale once initial documents are signed. In this case it put us in an appalling predicament. By then our own fairly heavy legal expenses on both properties would be lost and we should have to start all over again. Rightly or wrongly we decided to accept the reduced price, although this robbed us of working capital and caused us great distress.

In this case our pitiable lack of working capital was not seen as a good reason for investment by our local bank manager, and we started a period of crippling financial difficulties. When in Rome, live as the Romans! North Devon and particularly the Holsworthy area, was not at this time a very prosperous region. 'Mud and rushes' as one upcountry farmer described it. The holdings were usually small, around a hundred acres, and although milk production was the main income, this was usually achieved by milking the local Red Devon beef cattle, and occasionally the huge South Devons — at this time a dual purpose breed — until the fresh calved cows' milk had dropped to about a

116

gallon a day, when she was put back out in the fields with her calf, which had been retained in a pen with many others, and let out twice a day to strip the last of the milk from the udder.

At the time we arrived in the hamlet, only six or seven churns were awaiting the milk lorry on the communal milk stand, which served three farms and a very smallholder. Those taking milk up in the morning always had a surreptitious look at the labels, to see how well the neighbours were doing — and in a heat wave, what had been returned as sour!

In our area, the ancient farmhouses were all close by in the shelter of the hamlet, the land radiating out from this centre, each having a proportion of marsh — *mash* as it was pronounced. The marshland, truly all mud and rushes, came into its own in a dry season, when the cattle would take the rushes down to the roots, and a type of marsh grass would then spread like wildfire and be greedily devoured by the cattle. The upland fields close to the houses and buildings, had ancient permanent grass. This would yield two tons/acre of hay in a good season and in the wet seasons being well drained and deep rooted, could be heavily grazed without damaging the sward. The marshes which were burned every February, were home to snipe, woodcock and innumerable marsh birds of every variety.

On a February day a walk down to the marshes in the queer low yellow sunlight of this season, could easily lead you to believe you had been transported to the Everglades of Florida, the streams of lichen hanging off the alder, ash and bog oak, giving a queer green underwater look. The fields had all been carefully banked at one time, no doubt when there were large families of strong young sons on the land, the gateways framed up in stone, but in a wet season, the rushes stood eighteen inches high, looking a coarse unattractive feed.

It was very necessary for us to get some sort of income to live on and so with tiny capital we set off to Launceston market to find some dairy cattle. Holsworthy rarely had any breeds but Red Devons. Launceston frequently sold Ayrshires and Ayrshire crosses; these we felt would be able to cope with incessant wet conditions and still yield well, as we had not enough acres to go into beef. We had our own milk stand out of the hamlet and our neighbours, mostly helpful to a struggling young couple, were interested to know how much milk we expected to produce off our little place.

One childless lady, very scathing in her

assessment of us, had called up into the furniture lorry when Alan was unloading: 'Better put it all back again, it's no use you Londoners thinking you can make a living off that farm!' Later on when I met her in the hamlet, walking down with the baby in the pram, she reiterated her belief to me; when I told her I was not a Londoner, but Devon-born and bred from Exeter, she replied, 'Aw' Exeter!' in an air of absolute contempt as though it was a far country — which I suppose it was for her as I doubt if she had ever been farther than Bude in her whole life.

In our first trip to Launceston (Lanston as our neighbours pronounced it), we picked up four Ayrshire fresh calvers and two close to calving. These were duly delivered later in the day, and we put them into the three loose boxes at the top of the yard as the shippon, milking engine and pipes needed attention. The first morning I hand-milked, Alan staying in the house with the baby. From my perch on the stool, I looked across a valley to several hundred acres opposite. They were divided into several holdings, and it was fascinating to see the farming community starting their day. One farmer going out to work his land with a pair of horses, another taking his tractor and trailer into his sheep with a load of roots to feed them, a pair of collies bounding about beside him, further away cattle being called in. Looking far into the distance I could see the Dartmoor range, and North Hessary Tor which only appeared in very frosty weather or prior to rain.

Milking buckets and later machine-units were all loaded onto a bicycle to the farmhouse kitchen for sterilisation, and the churns of milk from the morning milking taken up to the stand, uncooled. The churn with the evening's milk yield in it, was kept separate and stood in a pan of water overnight. In the morning before its departure to the dairies, a brimming pint measure of cream was taken in for breakfast, a normal practice in our area, and despite this our butterfat percentage was never lower than 4.7%; the Ayrshires were not only good milkers but high in butterfat too.

Alan's duty was to go up to the yard and see the close-to-calving cows before going to bed, and then cycle up at 3 a.m. and have another look at her. Waking at 6 a.m. I found him still not home, rushing up to the buildings in a panic, the son and heir fast asleep, I was furious to find Alan sound asleep in a manger, with the proud mum licking her newly born heifer calf — he had slept right through the calving and was never trusted for the job again!

Down in the hamlet our neighbour Edwin looked doubtfully at our Ayrshires. 'Do you reckon them sparky (dairy) cows will live up here then?' We said that if they could survive in Scottish conditions, they ought to be able to make it here. Down in the hamlet the dark evenings were lit by the farmers and their families walking round feeding and milking their cows, hurricane lamps dangling from the prongs of their long-handled forks. The cattle were shoved into a variety of little stone or cob buildings and the names of the cows reflected this. There was Duckhouse cow, Twizzle tail, old Blind Faggoty, and so on.

If your man went out on one of these nefarious night pilgrimages, he was unlikely to return quickly, although it was possible that old Blindy might have kicked over the stool and stepped on him, it was much more likely that two or three men had gathered together for a 'Tell'. Alan was not immune to this and it was infuriating that when he disappeared to do some trifling errand, it might be hours before he got home. There was always plenty of gossip, and the whole area was run on a lease-lend principle.

The local population were staunch Methodists, and in any kind of emergency you were sure to be able to collect some help.

Some of us were very poor, and certainly none were what would be called today 'comfortably off'. If you had a bad season or were like us under-capitalised, you tightened your belts and could afford meat on only a few days each week. Tattie pastie was the order of the day, and the local wives managed to make it very appetising by slicing the potatoes very thin, seasoning well with plenty of salt and pepper, and then scalding the house ration of milk. The cream was added to the potato, and the skim used for tea. The pot being put back in the Rayburn oven with more water after use, for the next snack! The pastry had scarcely any fat in it, just a bit saved from the last roast, and was rolled very thin, so it was probably quite nutritious. Nobody was ever obese on these hardworking farms.

We all had a few hens and some of our neighbours had huge flocks, all on free range, perching at night in the high trees above the centre of the hamlet and the horse pond and milk stand. Their age was calculated by buying a new breed each year, the older ones always boiled for the household on the big cauldron over the inglenook fires. They were all very kind to Philip — Devon people always love children so it was a very happy place for him to grow up. Later on we got busier and busier on the farm, cutting overgrown hedges and banks, layering the roots and bringing back home wood fit for the fires, which our next door neighbour who used to bring his big diesel tractor back from work at the weekend, sawed up for us and the rest of the hamlet. Of course although we did not use faggots in our household having no inglenook open fire, these cut out and bound when hedging were a good bartering point in the community as they were essential for starting the hot ashes up every morning or even using the brick bread ovens beside the ingles.

I had had to make a very sad decision for myself. My dear little bitch, Bonnie, had always been jealous of Alan's appearance in my life. As Philip grew older and toddled about with us, I had a terrible premonition that one day she might bite him — she was not very keen on any men in her life although still devoted to me. As I mulled over these possibilities, Bonnie seemed to sense my concerns, and refused to leave my side. It was a terrible day for me when I asked Alan to take her to the Vet's and put her to sleep. This is the only time in my life when I have not held my canine friends in my arms when they had to have a lethal injection at the end of their lives. I felt so agonised over the whole decision that I knew that I would alarm her otherwise.

A month or two afterwards one of the daughters of the hamlet came round to my kitchen door with a litter of collie pups whose parents I had always admired. She asked me if I would like one as the rest were to be destroyed. I was so upset that I felt I could never have another dog again, after having betrayed Bonnie. She said she quite understood but that Alan had asked her to try me anyhow and please to choose the one I liked best as perhaps someone else would like him too. I blindly pointed to one, and rushed indoor to dry my tears. By the time the puppy was weaned, he was a handsome fellow of equable temperament like his dad, and we took him into the family and called him Simon. He was a wonderful dog and took the greatest care of Philip and later his brother, minding the pram like a nanny and learning to work our cows and later our horses.

As Alan and I got busier and busier on the farm as the herd built up, one of our neighbours used to push Philip out, who at the age of eleven months was walking already and very lively coming everywhere on the farm with us and Simon. This was in the afternoons after his nap. She and her family were desperately hard up, their tiny cottage was nearly derelict, and the roof had fallen in upstairs, and remained that way all the time we were there. She very sweetly polished and cleaned her little kitchen for Phil's arrival, the kitchen table scrubbed white, the little range black-leaded with the brass work polished, and the slate flag-stones (which we all had) washed and cleaned with skim milk, and polished until they shone. Her husband who was undertaker/carpenter used to help Alan with any building jobs on the farm and was not too proud to tell us when we left, that the very little we could afford to pay them both, had made all the difference to their weekly housekeeping. Their help to us at this time, would never be forgotten either.

11

It was not long before our need for more cows to push up the milk sales, led us to sell the V8 gas-guzzler, and then I caught the bus into Holsworthy on market day to buy fish for Philip, meat and some extras, I could not get at the local stores. On market day the square was always packed, as apart from the cattle market there were stalls of every sort in the square, some with lovely Devon-made pottery ware, and being seconds, very cheap. As I went into the bank for weekly cash, there were queues of farmers waiting to see the bank manager; times were very hard, and overdrafts were hard to come by and even harder to keep. There was a long line of cattle sticks with calf-muzzles attached, which their owners left in the lobby, showing that they had brought a cow or two to sell, and the milk had been withheld from the calf until after sale to show the cow's udder to advantage. Nearly all the farmer's wives brought in pasties, butter and cream, eggs and dressed fowls, in their market baskets, which they would exchange for the week's meat ration and the extras they could not produce at home.

The local bakery I remember had a large sign outside advertising factory-made cakes. These were satisfyingly gooey for those of us who lived on economically home-baked scones and sponge cakes. I and Phil always had one with a cup of tea at the restaurant section whilst waiting for the bus to take us home.

Our finances were incredibly precarious and in order to avoid having a nervous breakdown or manic depression, we had evolved a system of doing our accounts one evening a month, after the arrival of the monthly milk cheque. The bills for cattle feed, fodder and vets etc were clipped together after the arrival of the post every morning at the ridiculous hour of six a.m., a tremendous walloping being given to the door by our postman who had a sadistic satisfaction in hearing this wake the baby. Suitably fortified by high tea and before evening milking — we did not want sleepless nights — we then went systematically through the list of creditors settling what we could to the extent the milk cheque allowed and the tiny amount for our housekeeping, and the rest had to wait until next month or a bonus such as the sale of bull-calves and so on. Any very stroppy creditor was firmly put down the line!

We were soon not without our own transport to market as one of our farmer neighbours had just got the money together to buy a car, a great ambition of his and his wife. Unfortunately he had never learned to drive and so struck a bargain with Alan, that Alan would drive us all to market, and come back after the cattle and sheep sales were over for the day (in very good time in our area, for everyone to get home to the late afternoon farm chores) The car lived out in the yard and on one occasion a broody hen on eggs had to be chucked out first! She had climbed in through an open window.

We were able to borrow a horse and cart to spread basic slag on the grass in early spring. The bags were tipped up into the dung cart on a calm dry day, and the fertilizer thrown out systematically, as in corn sowing, with a firepan (an ordinary fireside shovel). The unfortunate man in the back doing the distribution (Alan of course) was black as a sweep at the end of the day, for there is always a little breeze on the warmest spring day in North Devon.

Most of the local farmers grew a little acreage of feeding oats for their stock, the oat straw being fed to the stock, the horses given a sheaf of corn to sort out for themselves. In each hamlet somehow we all got our sheaves into a rick near the house. During the winter the thresher toured the area and every man in the hamlet helped to thresh. The men took this very easily for indeed some days there was only a few hours work, which could have taken half a day.

The women however had to put on the most enormous 'threshing spread' in their kitchens starting at 10 a.m., 12 o'clock lunch and then finally an enormous cooked tea. I was horrified at the idea! All the women had numerous female relatives who turned up to help at this important social occasion and in any case they were cooking and preparing delicacies to vie with neighbours' efforts, days ahead. I was busy with milking and mucking out and had no female help, Mrs J. my childminder being far too valuable for me to ask her to undertake extra duties. At that time no macho Devon farmer was ever expected to carry a dish or help domestically, although I planned to waylay Alan off the stack and get something carried in by him.

To my chagrin, after organising the whole event — Alan succumbed to one of his all too regular migraines and had to retire to bed. I was left alone to cope — of course he wasn't missed at all on the thresher as our acreage of oats was minute! And took only an hour or two to thrash. I used to dope Alan up with plenty of aspirin in our early years when any kind of pressure could bring on attacks. Later on great publicity was given to the harmful effects of aspirin on the stomach and digestive systems; for many years I blamed myself for possibly wrecking his long-term health, but in the way of these things the wheel has now turned full circle, and in the last ten years aspirin has received considerable respect from the medical profession, and cardiac patients are now being dosed with it long-term, to thin the blood so maybe I did right after all!

Living in our little Devon hamlet was an eye-opener after rural life in West Surrey. As our neighbour provided us with transport I in return showed his young daughter how to dress make, and together we found patterns and material from the market stalls. I ran her up some pretty dresses for her chapel socials, but I had to chuckle that on Sundays when the lay preacher might unexpectedly make a visit, Edwin's wife would take her darning upstairs as this work would be frowned upon. Naturally in our hamlet, no female sat down and did nothing. Of course the males had a quite different ethos.

When any chapel social was planned, all

the women had a terrific cooking splurge to make sure there were sufficient refreshments. If there were any sandwiches left over, they were liable to be carefully packed under a clean cloth, and when one of the rota chapel cleaners came up, they might be sprinkled with water to keep them fresh for a mid-week meeting.

One of the daughters of our neighbouring farmers was to be married. Her dress carefully picked from a Bideford shop had to have a few alterations made (the bride-to-be's waistline had enlarged of recent weeks). To very great consternation the package failed to arrive in the post. The shop was adamant that it had been posted, and unwilling to replace it. It was pure luck that the youngest daughter, chasing errant hens' nests, chanced to look in a huge ancestral harvest wagon in the Linhay, a great favourite of the birds, and found a very soiled package which had been tossed in by our postman (he of the mighty fist); when he failed to find anyone indoors, he had then gone off on leave!

In the quieter parts of the countryside in the 50s there were still plenty of real 'characters'. Television had not encroached on the local individuality with the plastic characters of the popular 'soaps'. Alec was one of the rapidly diminishing race of genuine

English eccentrics. He was an individualist, one of those happy mortals who did not let moral issues deflect him from living a life free as air.

Originally he hailed from 'Up Lunnon way'. Somewhere about the time of the national call-up in 1939 he appeared in the district looking for farm work. As labour was always scarce in such an under-populated district of family farms, there were always numerous jobs waiting for him, and usually a barn or stable to spare for his accommodation. It was of course useless to expect an early start from Alec. His first requirement was an enormous breakfast, to be served about 8.30 a.m. If unable to rouse him at this hour, all that was necessary was to open the kitchen window and allow the aroma of grilled bacon to percolate through the yard. It worked like magic!

He was popular with farmers' wives because although his food intake was terrific, they paid him out of their egg money, to do all those little jobs their husbands could never been induced to undertake. Attention to the strengthening of washing lines, cleaning out the coal shed, chopping logs and a hundred other wearisome duties that everyone else had excellent excuses to avoid. He had a streak of good nature which made him enjoy helping a farmer or perhaps motorist in distress, spending hours on his back in the cold and mud, and then rewarded with a tip, would wave thanks away with a deprecatory gesture, to depart with the best of the unfortunate's tools lining his pockets.

He once boasted that he knew the inside of every police station in a forty mile radius, and a good percentage of those on his usual hitch-hiking route to London, which he visited at frequent intervals dictated by the amount of wages he had managed to accumulate. His few possessions were mortgaged with local employers when the urge to 'visit relations' overcame him. This was not so foolish of them as might appear at first sight. Alec, returning hungry and penniless a few weeks later, would work magnificently to reclaim his bike, which was needed to get him a drink at the nearest pub, seven miles away.

Alec worked a small area which he had found by experience to contain the very kindest-hearted small farmers. Crime being very unusual in this area, the police soon looked Alec up if anything was reported missing. These visitations were however bad for Alec's nerves, and he was apt to get away from it all by visiting his relations — who were of course mythical — until a little bird told him that investigations were now abandoned, when once again he would return unheralded, bearing small presents for whichever family his possessions were mortgaged with at the time.

Although living rough Alec managed to shave almost as often as his most respectable employers, and at times looked no more than his thirty-five years. He had a mania for tidiness, an asset to any farm, and his talents also included drain clearing and chimney sweeping — the latter in our area mainly consisted of climbing to the top of the roof and dropping a large holly bush with a barn weight attached, down the inglenook chimneys. On a wet day he could be seen about the district carrying out small ditching projects gratis, merely it seemed, for the pleasure of watching the water running freely. One day having been dispatched by one of his numerous employers with a set of chimney brushes to the house of an aged relative living some miles away, he managed to make the job last three days, having contracted to sweep every chimney en route for five shillings at time, plus meals.

Admittedly light-fingered, Alec had the sweet and trusting nature of a child. It never occurred to him that he might be 'done by as you did'! It came as the saddest disillusionment, therefore, when on two occasions I know of, the tables were turned on him. It happened this way. Edwin having a large yardful of muck to be carted endeavoured to contract Alec for the job. Alec, strong as an ox, knew his value to the farmer to the last penny, and demanded a new pair of rubber boots before starting the job. Resignedly Edwin bought these for him, then having wasted the morning in town with him gave him a large dinner and after three and a half hours' work, an equally large tea. After promises to start in the yard earlier than usual next morning it is not surprising that the farmer was enraged to hear from his son that Alec had moved off in the night! Having made some enquiries in the district Edwin tracked him down, and late the following night visited his new accommodation.

He found him peacefully asleep in the hay under a Dutch barn. Withdrawing silently, he noted the new boots standing in their newly washed lustre on a bale, and decided to take them with him. When Alec awoke to discover the theft he was furious, for his new, and far easier job, entailed washing out pigsties, for which boots were essential. Even worse was in store for Alec, one night after cycling into a large market town some twenty miles away for a celebration at the noisiest pub in town. He came out at closing time to discover someone had actually stolen his Dynamo lighting set off his bike. 'And on my Birthday too,' he cried reproachfully — 'When I were standing all me pals a round, I paid for that there lamp out of my wages!'

We had a strange introduction to another local character, Harry Jones, a local Cattle dealer. We decided to accompany our surplus bull calves taken to our local market by a haulier up the road who was collecting livestock whose owners were too busy at home, or had no transport like us. We had been quite unable to understand why our several previous bull calves, fine strong upstanding specimens had been rejected by the calf auctioneers and labelled as bobbies (of manufacturing value only). Having arrived to find our two calves strangely penned away from the main bunch where obviously the market foreman was engaged in a little fiddle, Alan had a serious talk to the market supervisor to make sure this never happened again — one reason why farmers always went regularly to market to see their stock sold.

Then whilst we were there we thought we would have a look round the milking cattle for sale. We were surprised to find a most unusually fine shorthorn cow, her udder bursting with milk. As I was handling her udder and trying the teats to see if she was an easy milker, Harry appeared on the scene and told me that she was blind in one quarter, therefore only a three quartered cow. I felt sure that this was nonsense as the quarter was soft, of even size and full of milk. I was pretty sure that she might have a tiny infection of the teat canal, which could be cleared at worst, by the passing of a catheter.

Anyhow we decided not withstanding we would bid for her as she was such a good type of animal, and being from upcountry and independent by nature we saw no reason to ask Jones to buy her for us, the established practice; leading to a commission for him. This was definitely against local rules and when she came into the auction ring, Harry did his stuff in front of all the buyers by stooping down, trying the udder and pronouncing to all and sundry that she had lost a quarter. I was surprised at the time that the vendor was not present to refute this accusation; subsequent events showed why he was silent.

Anyhow Alan and Harry took up the bidding to £73, quite a high price for a three quartered cow. Harry was obviously unused to anyone challenging him in this way, but he was a good sport and wished us well with our purchase. When we got her home I started to milk out the overstocked udder by hand, massaging the distended quarter with the blocked teat. To my amazement there was a sudden ping on the side of the bucket, and a tiny grain of wheat shot out of the teat. The vendor had blocked up her teats with seed wheat to stop her running her milk, and stock her udder up to a great size for sale! This cow turned out to be a wonderful milker and we headed the *Dairy Farmer Magazine* competition for the heaviest yielding cow of the week for many issues. It was not long after the sale that Harry popped in to see us and enquire about the shorthorn. Later on he sent in a few beasts he had bought in markets for us to keep for him, until he had a customer for them. I think he admired our cheek in standing up to him, and realised that we were struggling for our existence.

With such a high rainfall, some sixty inches per annum under Dartmoor, the local oat straw was very weathered and of poor feeding value. We could grow wonderful root crops, turnips on the ridge in the wettest fields. Rape was another heavy cropper and high in protein, despite its reputation for causing cows to slip their calves. We decided to get maintenance plus two gallons from this, combined with oat straw, which we decided to buy from the Eastern counties. When our straw arrived in the hamlet on a gigantic lorry and trailer, our neighbours who turned out to have a look, could hardly believe their eyes, as the wonderful golden bales, unmarked by rain, shone in the autumn sunshine.

We milked at a twelve-hour interval 7 a.m. to 7 p.m. and after the evening milking we offered water in a bucket to every cow from our rainwater butt beside the Shippon roof. Our shorthorn would put away three buckets (ten gallons) every night, but she yielded eight gallons a day under our management. We were never without water in the buildings, because the iron roof gathered dew at night all summer long.

A farm is a marvellous place for a child to grow up. Philip used to ride on my knee when I drove the old standard Fordson, and when I brought back a wonderful old converted horse-turner from a sale for £2, derided by Alan at first as it needed someone on the back to kick the gears on and off by foot, but generally agreed to be the most efficient hay processor ever, Phil was able to sit on my knee and watch the swathes of hay roll under us. A farmer's wife has to be able to administer refreshment from a basket at all seasons to men working outside in either extreme heat or cold. A thermos is a poor substitute for a real pot of tea and handmade sandwiches and buns. I discovered that tea in the pot which had been milked and sugared, would stay warm for ages, wrapped in a towel, and so wherever Alan was working in the fields we would go and find him, and make a little picnic for us all. When the weather was warm and we had a car, we would run down to Northcote Mouth and with the car parked on the salted grass beside the pebble beach, we would dash into the breakers for a quick dip and a picnic to follow. There were no caravans or fences in those days and very few holidaymakers either so it was a private pleasure for us all.

Philip, who had gone on a visit to Alan's parents with him, had been lovingly entertained by his brother who initiated him into the delights of a garden tap and hose. These were delights he never had at home because water was far too valuable to waste. One afternoon I was busy in my little kitchen when it occurred to me to look out of the window where a veritable river of our precious TVO tractor fuel was deluging down our drive, Philip having turned on the brass tap of the oil tank which was alas! within child reach of a determined climber. This was an expense we could ill afford and so I suppose I might have had the imagination to see that this lively kid would not be stopped by a locked stable door of the barn.

One day doing my hand-wash, it occurred to me that there was an ominous quiet and rushing out into the garden (I knew he had not gone far because I had a view over the drive!) I made my way round to the barn to see a collection of wooden boxes and logs under the door. Philip had climbed up this erection, swarmed over the door, and was having a wonderful time pulling out all the coloured wires of our little generator! This had to be jettisoned as we could not afford to have it mended and so went back to oil lamps again.

Fortunately for us after we had been in the hamlet a year or two, the local blacksmith (as alternative electrician) was asked by the neighbouring parish village hall committee if he could light the hall for a very special event. To our delight he came to see us and offered to take our generator and overhaul it for us free, if they could have the loan of it for a few days. After this we had electric light again, but although the last light turned off at the bedside was supposed to automatically turn the generator off, we would lie waiting to hear if it had done this, or more usually the revs would go up like an angry beehive and one of us had to go down and do it ourselves.

New Forest ponies off to Germany

Janet Steele riding-in New Forest,
four-year-old mare

Ramblers Selina and Sonia,
Surrey County Show

12

Cider making turned out to be a great social gathering in the hamlet. No one had any proper orchards, but we all had a few gnarled old trees which seldom yielded any really decent eating apples; however in 1952 the apple crop was heavier than everyone could deal with, so we all bagged up our surplus apples in early autumn including the windfalls and at an appointed time the five families shared a tractor and trailer and made their way up to the Barton a few miles distant in the next parish, to use their ancient cider press. As fourteen sacks of apples are required to fill one hogshead (sixty gallons), there was a very large load of apples and barrels including sundry women and kids to transport in the 'dimsey' light of the early autumn evening. The whole scene being lit by hurricanes had the atmosphere of bygone ages. When I went out to see if I could help in the loading of the trailer I was alarmed to see many of the sacks oozing with rotten apples, which everyone assured me made the best brew. Prompt at seven that evening there was a great revving of car engines, as the convoy got under way.

The room housing the ancient and very simple machinery was very much in keeping with this centuries' old method, the walls roughly whitewashed, cobbles on the floor. The first operation was to pulp the apples in a machine similar to the ordinary root pulper. This one had a concession to modernity in that a petrol engine replaced the laborious hand labour, which had previously been necessary to turn the grinders. As the pulp fell to the floor, it was placed by hand over clean straw on the press. This was a heavy square tray of wood, set at a slight angle to the ground, with a narrow channel running round it, to convey the apple juice to a lip at the front, under which was placed a receiving vessel. Two large threaded metal uprights about six feet high, supported the remainder of the press, which was similarly shaped and screwed down by hand.

I cannot imagine how we all avoided food poisoning; it was a Health and Food Inspector's worst nightmare. There was no sterilisation of the press's channel or lip and it appeared to have had rodents running over it since the last brew went through! I can only assume that the fermentation process is mighty powerful in sterilising the brew because I never heard of anyone being ill after drinking this, only slightly hazy! There are many ideas as to how the straw should be laid on the press, but the general practice is to draw straight straw across two sides at right angles, the pulp is then built up and further straw added at intervals, the overlapping straws of the underneath section being brought over the pulp to secure the 'cheese' as it is called. This process is then repeated many times until the cheese reaches the top of the press.

The real fun then commenced. The hand screws of the press are turned by the strongest men, and with a delightful trickling sound the cider starts to run. So do the men in charge of filling the barrels; no time then for gossiping, but steady bailing into buckets, from which it was strained into the barrels, through a wooden box-funnel, which is filled with straw. As the flow ceased the press is lifted again and the cheese, which by now had been squeezed out of its original shape, is restored to its original dimensions with a knife, the overlap being placed on top for another squeeze. After this had been repeated two or three times, the cheese appeared dry and an enormous wooden spanner of about five foot in length was brought from some furthest recess of the old building and used to get the maximum pressure from the press.

At length the end of the cider flow was reached, only a tiny heap of dry straw pulp left of the original huge heap. This much fancied by the hamlet's pigs and cattle and of though no specific feeding value gave the beasts a merry time! Pigs and cattle over-indulging in this tasty fare were liable to be found rolling drunk! By the end of the evening's labours, the hour is late, the company in good humour (all having sampled to their satisfaction the sweet and innocent flavoured new brew); it was only fifteen minutes after having imbibed that the strength hit you. Advice gets a little hazy and we were not sure if the tip about putting the week's bacon ration into the barrel is a leg pull or not so compromised by adding raw beetroot and preservative into to the barrel.

Once home the hogsheads required considerable manpower to steer their course through doors, down passages and stairs to their working positions. They were left on their sides with the bung hole open. It takes many days to work a barrel, the cleansing action of the fermentation forcing out any impurities or foreign matter, and many bottles of cider are needed to top up the barrel while this is taking place. Eventually came the day when the barrel mounted on a stand, the tricky two-man job of tapping takes place, the bung being drawn instantaneously with the insertion of the tap. Truly one may say 'no bungling' here: sixty gallons of cider pouring itself all over the floor is no joke!

However when the whole operation was completed, and my deepest suspicions about all types of peasant wines confirmed, I endeavoured to forget the lack of female food hygiene in the whole affair and we were very happy to offer our first attempt to make rough cider to our visiting friends. It was a howling success: sweet, clear and amber, it had the liveliness of champagne, combined with a guarantee to make troubles fly far away after a second glass. We had several farming friends from out of the area to entertain. Pat and Jim from Bideford way were expert winemakers; their elderflower champagne was hard to beat and their gin a literal knock over. However we held our own with our cider, though we have never made it again.

Now that our dairy herd was increasing, it was time to consider what we could do to make the family farm easier to manage and more lucrative. It was obvious that living so far from the shippons, was not really satisfactory. We decided that we would build a modest bungalow beside our farm buildings, and from its living room and bedrooms the marvellous panorama of the north-west outline of the Dartmoor Tors would be framed, as a background to our precious herd. Having obtained planning permission, which was not so difficult in the fifties, provided we could produce our own adequate water supply, we then found a builder, which was not so easy in the agricultural area. He had no doubts that he could build us a nice house within the given estimate, so before going any further we put the farmhouse, its outbuildings and four acres of paddock into the market, and most surprisingly sold it immediately.

After our first house sale we were not going to be caught out again by any dodgy dealings at the final stage of contract exchange. Putting our furniture in store in one of our buildings, our builder friend reckoned that it would be only a month or two before he could have us installed, even if some finishing work had to be done around us. As we were now in September, it seemed feasible to hire a caravan quite cheaply for the winter let and place it adjacent to the milking parlour conversion of our shippon, which now included a nice little yard paved with the biggest of the flat stones from Bude beach which the Council were always happy to sell, set in lightly brushed home-mixed concrete and strong enough to take any heavy traffic we could use on it. The herd was now fifteen-cow-strong, and we reared our own pedigree heifers as herd replacements.

The summer prior to this we had taken one of our yearling heifers to all the local shows with great success, I leading her and very pleased to be back in business again in the show ring. As the classes were for mixed dairy breeds, we found ourselves having the temerity to show against an extremely prosperous north Devon Friesian breeder.

When our heifer beat his in front of a well known judge, this gentleman was absolutely hopping mad. And puce in the face confronted Alan saying that he had paid £400 for her only a month ago, and did not expect to be beaten by the likes of us! It was not only stupid of him because our heifer, though home-bred, was out of a very good pedigree cow, and of course I had not forgotten my old expertise in trimming and exhibiting her! And in any case in any mixed breed class be it canine, equine or bovine it is largely luck as to whether the judge favours your own breed! But belonging to a smallholder as she did — oh dear!

During these pleasant showing days, with Philip staked out in his pram and pram harness at the end of the cattle lines — he was expert as a lively toddler in standing up in pram harness and rocking the boat so we had to use a fencing post to keep it from tipping over, and with a stack of toys kept for the day was happy and warm in his well-sprung, boat-shaped pram, and I must say I do not envy today's babies and toddlers in their most uncomfortable, unsprung, cold buggies.

Unfortunately I began to feel rather sick and had unpleasant stomach pains. Of course if you were of child-bearing age in those days, your troubles were always put down to pregnancy. However after some weeks of discomfort I had another go at the doctor's surgery and this time he said why on earth hadn't I come in before because this was appendicitis and acute and if I didn't go in at once to the Stratton Hospital at Bude to have an operation, I should be risking peritonitis. This was very inconvenient as it meant leaving Alan single-handed with milking and cattle, together with the baby. However I must say that I was able on the state to have the best-managed operation ever at this nice little hospital, where I was able to sit out in the pretty gardens to convalesce.

By the time our sale was well advanced I was well again and we motored over to Westward Ho to interview the proprietors of the big caravan park there. In July and August parked beside the sea, they were filled with happy, laughing, suntanned holidaymakers, hung about with bright bathing costumes and towels and blaring radios. Now they stood, closed up, dreary and deserted for the new season's tenants to inspect. Another type altogether, sensibly clad against strong sea, gales and muddy ground, they haggled with the owners for a cheap winter rent, fairly sure that with a good reference they will have their home for a fraction of the summer rent, merely for keeping it aired, beating the damp, salty winter atmosphere which played havoc with the furnishings.

In due course a streamlined four-berth caravan arrived and was pulled into its allotted space. A home on wheels — what romance in the words. Oh sad reality! Our double-berth appeared to have been made for a pair of pigmies, three foot six wide and only five foot six long it was a source of agony to a six foot five man and a wife built on similar lines. The toddler fitted into his double-berth very nicely, but as he retired at six p.m. we were obliged to draw the snappy little wooden partition across the centre of the van, which allowed us a small box of about five foot six square in which to cook and eat our supper, dig the bedclothes from under the seat and make the bed, and then cleverly do the accounts on the draining board-cum-table, when the supper was washed up.

There was of course also the matter of the hinged dining table which collapsed regularly under the weight of our massive intake of food, utterly unlike the hasty summer meals of a holiday family. The dainty little wardrobe which refused to encompass our utility farm garb and the lack of a hook, or place to put one, on which to hang a wringing wet mac or overcoat. Rubber boots, the curse of all farm wives, were taken off on the step, and thrown under the van where they reposed soaking up the damp autumn air, to be recovered on one's stomach in the early hours of the morning dank and horrid for early milking. As autumn dwindled into winter our bungalow was still incomplete, and now even our workmen disappeared, to tackle priority work, they assured us. By this time the winter gales swung the caravan at night so that we rolled about in our bunks for all the world like a ship crossing the bay. Frantically sleepless in the small hours I would wonder if the chains securing our caravan to the yard, would endure, or if we would blow back to Surrey, from whence we had come, four years before.

By this time condensation was a curse; the walls streamed nightly despite the absence of skylight ventilators, which blew away regularly. How I envied the cows lying in their commodious quarters ministered so carefully by us as we lived damp, cold and dirty in our home on wheels. Alan had to go away for a few days; it was the deal that whichever of us went on holiday, had to take Philip with them. I was left to cope with the farm. Miraculously the weather changed to calm, dry, moonlight nights. Alone and in some degree of comfort after work, the poultry started to be a nuisance. The turkeys would insist on perching on top of the van and as our furniture was occupying their winter quarters I had no alternative for them. Meanwhile the geese discovered they could find shelter under the van. Nothing would deflect these two parties once they had discovered the comfort of caravans for poultry.

On a moonlit night (conditions which are always upsetting for poultry) the noise was dreadful. Half dazed with sleep I would emerge with the inevitable gumboots and stick, and in my night attire proceed to drive my cackling flock of horrors, into the paddock from which they had escaped. After the removal of the geese, the turkeys on the roof would settle down and apart from the occasional one or two slipping off in a gust of wind, whence they noisily tried to regain their favourite position, the night would pass reasonably quietly.

Just before Christmas one of the Ayrshires spotted Simon sleeping outside the van door. For some reason only known to her, she was convinced that he was responsible for her separation from her newly born son. Swiftly she plunged at the dog, who smartly leaped under the van for shelter. A ghastly crash ensued and as I came round the corner to investigate, there was the most enormous hole in the side of the van! Of course the sides were only a type of strong cardboard as we informed the owners when we handed the thing over to them in early spring when the vans were needed back at the summer site and anyhow we had kept the confounded thing well aired for them!

13

I was by April absolutely sick of caravan living. We were then waiting for plasterers to complete the bungalow, so Alan clad the cob walls of the old dairy in good clean plaster board and we moved in there in comparative comfort, having partitioned off a little space for Philip's cot. The only problem occurred when we decided to dishorn the herd later in the month, just as an unusually warm, dry spell arrived. Several of the horn sites became infested with maggots and twice a day, had to be syringed out with hydrogen peroxide, a very gruesome, smelly job when living on the spot, so to speak.

Fortunately our new well held out in the dry spell, and we could always get beautiful water from a spring half way down one of our fields. This came out of a clay pipe, but so deep it was considered unsuitable for grant purposes, whereas our well-site found by a diviner was a fully granted supply for dairy and house. When we called in the local water diviner he arrived with a modest hazel twig cut from the hedge. Two turns around the building site and then suddenly the twig

The boys, with three unexpected arrivals

turned in the old man's hand with such force, that it tore the skin off one of his fingers. Twenty foot down he said positively, sticking the stick firmly in the ground; a nod of approval from the Ministry man meant that work could commence, and we would be able to receive a 50% grant towards the cost. Our diviner being a public-spirited man was quite happy to let us have a try with the stick, just in case we had the gift, but sadly nothing happened with us.

With the absence of drilling machines at that time, hand-digging was the order of the day, and with the tenacity of a couple of moles, the well-diggers disappeared in the direction indicated. Twenty feet down, work was stopped by an impenetrable layer of rock, and still no water — undeterred the Ministry man ordered that the rock should be blown with a charge. So a hole was drilled in this rock layer and the dynamite inserted. After this we retreated behind the nearest bank, and after the explosion five anxious faces peered into twenty feet of dust and smoke and waited. As the air cleared, behold! water was bubbling through the fissured rock and our supply and 50% grant was assured! It now required lining with concrete rings, the installation of a pump, and house building could begin.

Although we had cured the rat problem in our last farmhouse, word had got round the rat population that the shippon was worth a visit, because after the evening milking, the milk filter was squeezed into a saucer for the cat and the wool ball thrown into the straw of the dung channel, which was cleaned out in the morning. At one time the rats got very bold and coming up the drainage pipe at the bottom of the shippon, they would whip up the squeezer wool and carry it back down the drain with them. Alan was very quick and with youthful precision waited for the rat to come out and leaped on him as he made off with his treat — killing him with his hob-nailed boots. A few rat droppings on top of the cow cake bin in the morning showed we had had visitors in the night! Taking all the cow cake out except for a tempting six inches in the bottom we left the bin open. In the morning mother and eight nearly full-grown babies were held captive in the bottom, being unable to climb the sides of the slippery metal bin. These were polished off with a heavy stick, used like a food blender.

Of course with soft red earth banks everywhere, rats were always waiting to take advantage of any opportunity to come out of the holes and raid the farmer's buildings. However by being very clean and tidy with feeding stuffs and farmyard management, it is not too difficult to dissuade them, and encourage them to move on. Of course collie dogs are quite useless with vermin, as they have no killing instinct at all, and will run around a stationary pheasant or rabbit in a field as they are sent to bring in the stock.

Whilst we were living in the dairy our builder made it clear that he was not returning to finish the house. Unfortunately we were naive enough to have fallen for his plea for more money upfront to hire the plasterers which of course failed to turn up after many weeks of waiting. It was clear that he had made off with our cash and we would have to finish the house ourselves. Fortunately Alan's brother was between jobs and wives and promised to come down and help us out. Although we could not plaster ourselves we used plasterboard taping the joints and covering with heavy woodchip paper; it was really quite effective.

Eventually Alan and Peter got round to filling the drainage ditch by hand, so that in getting to the outside loo bucket in the dark I did not fall in the holes on the way which was very necessary as I was by then pregnant again having decided to have a second child by the time Philip was four years old, so that he could enjoy the new arrival's company without the terrible jealousy that younger siblings can suffer. We were still buying and selling cows and we had an interesting example of the human aspect of the pre-technical era in the quiet rural area around us. We decided to sell a very nice fresh-calved Ayrshire cow at Hatherleigh market, which at that time had some considerable local demand for good quality pedigree dairy cows. Naturally with the expense of finishing our house, some extra cash was needed for bathroom and kitchen equipment, so we entered one of our most showy cows who had to be watched carefully whilst the machine was put on her, as she was inclined to wipe the cluster off with her hind feet in the first minute or two. Her calf accompanied her but was sold to a different buyer.

We were surprised to hear from the auctioneer that the purchaser complained that we had sold him a vicious animal. I explained that as a mere female I always milked her on my own and if she had a back rope to hold the cluster on she was easily milked. However the man created a stink and we said that he could bring her back and cancel the sale. This he did but of course by then the cow was very unsettled and missed her calf in the confusion of travelling home again. Turned out in the best pasture with the other old biddies, she was absent when they came in for the morning milking. It was indeed almost impossible to see where she had got out of the field — she must have climbed a steep bank and wandered into a neighbour's field and from thence out on to the lane.

Naturally we searched for her high and low. She was a very distinctly marked sparky cow and as such very recognisable as she had a lot of white on her and a huge udder, a very unlikely candidate for straying. Nobody had seen her for miles around, we called at every farm in the parish — asked the postman, the post office and even went over the main Bideford — Holsworthy road, when a visiting postman said he had seen a similar cow heading north up a lane the week before. We were frantic; this good cow was giving five gallons of milk per day and worth a very substantial price (our new bathroom and kitchen in fact) — her loss was enormous to us.

One morning speaking to one of our Bideford friends on the phone, I told her of our loss — at this point the operator intervened and told me that she had heard someone mention that a Mr X of Honeymead had got a wonderful cow he had found on the road! Sure enough when we found the smallholding, a dear old pensioner and his wife were enjoying a fantastic addition to their dairy, the *dangerous* cow had been hand milked for the last *ten days* by a very crippled man who walked with two sticks, he and his wife having made pounds of butter and cream meanwhile!

Straying animals are a real nuisance and this was the only cow we ever owned that legged it from the herd, however Alan and I, visiting a farm dispersal in Cornwall where they had a very nice pedigree Ayrshire herd, found eight lovely show-quality bulling heifers which we thought would be a sensible investment (we used good AI bulls from the Torrington centre at that time). These turned out to be the most awful bunch of straying animals we have ever had to deal with *nothing* kept them in. We tried every means at our disposal to restrain them but alas! they had been ranched at their former home and ran along the top of the banks, jumping any wire or obstruction in their way. Straying stock make bad neighbours, even though they were sympathetic to us in our dilemma, and suggested putting wooden yokes around their necks, so they could not squeeze through any weak places; this was not a success.

Naturally they did not want tracks through

their growing cornfields so one day with one of our neighbours to help us, we drove them into our substantial block-built boxes, and drove the door bolts across. Congratulating each other we all stood red-faced and gasping at our efforts. There was an enormous crash as they all burst out through the closed and apparently impenetrable wooden doors! Eventually they were recaptured and we promised their imminent departure before we were excommunicated. Fortunately there was an Ayshire collective sale at Reading quite shortly, so Alan entered them in this, in four matching pairs — they were very beautiful — leaving Peter and I and Philip on the farm, Alan booked a railway truck at the station to take them direct to the sale to arrive at six in the morning, to give them plenty of time to be washed off for sale. Then he went up by passenger train to join them. When he got there they had not arrived — (eventually he discovered that the truck had been labelled for repair and shunted off to a siding at Wanborough near Guildford, some bright spark having put the wrong ticket on it!)

Eventually it arrived after the start of the sale, two of the auctioneers' drovers having helped him drive them from the station to the market sale yard. Of course they were filthy and were unable to be washed for sale. Alan had arranged for them to be sold in the catalogued pairs, as he felt that these heifers would probably settle better if the group was split up and going to several purchasers. Actually despite their grubby appearance they sold moderately well. After their sale the buyer contacted Alan and said he liked them so much he had bought the lot — he was cautioned to put them in wire-meshed captivity.

During the sale there was an announcement to the effect that an outbreak of foot-and-mouth disease imposed restrictions on any cattle being moved in an eastward direction, causing an instant drop in the prices of dairy cows. Alan decided to turn a disappointment over our bulling-heifers into a positive bargain and purchase four milk-recorded dairy cows very cheaply, putting them in the hands of the Great Western railway, the auctioneers arranging their dispatch after milking them out, and leading them down to the truck Alan had just commissioned. Ringing me up in great spirits from his parents — he was staying up there a few days — he gave me the catalogue details. One cow said to be recorded as giving six gallons a day. The station rang me early next morning to say the cows were in, and a haulier was there to deliver them to us.

164

Peter and I then had a chance to find out about the cows Alan had bought for us. The high yielder gave almost nothing, and when we examined her ear, the vendors, a well-known Educational Trust farm had sent the wrong cow! In the efficient way we were accustomed to at that time, Thimbleby & Shorland intervened with the vendor for us and we received full and acceptable compensation. The cow that they had substituted (nicknamed Bugger-Lugs by Peter) was a real stinker with the ability to make milking a real battle. We coped with our four new arrivals with a vow to make the purchaser see for himself what he had sent us, when he returned from his holiday!

Gradually the new bungalow was completed, the drive beach-pebbled and our furniture recovered from mouldy storage. Peter having shown me how to wallpaper I took over this part of the job joyfully, and though by now I was pretty bulky managed to get all the rooms quite pretty.

Alan had bought us a little van from the local feed merchants and her previous driver used to pat her bonnet affectionately as he made his delivery in the new and bigger vehicle, explaining her little foibles to me. Though a tricky starter I found practically no compression when I started her by handle

— much like a sewing machine! I loved her dearly and the freedom she gave me was a wonderful boon.

We kept a lot of turkeys free-range and looking for nests used to be Philip's little task. One day struggling over the threshold triumphantly bearing a cap full of eggs (worth three shillings and six pence each for setting, a vast sum to us at that time) he managed to trip up and lost the lot in the biggest scrambled egg ever prepared — diluted by copious tears! Our senior stag turkey was a fantastic bird over 25 pounds in weight, his wattles flaming scarlet and purple. Alan loathed him, which he reciprocated by attacking him from behind whenever he crossed the yard. The junior stag was a very inferior individual who dared not announce himself with glowing colours, but was soberly dressed and allowed only the odd hen to keep him quiet.

After Peter left us I thought I had better go up to Surrey to get my teeth fixed, before the new baby's arrival became too imminent. I never trusted the local dentist at that time after having paid a visit and been asked, 'Which one do you want pulled?' After my departure with Philip, Alan gave vent to his feelings, when the big stag attacked him while crossing the yard. Carrying a large stem of

Kale for protection, he threw it at him and caught him on the head. To his horror Sonia's precious bird collapsed in a heap at his feet! Looking green about the gills it allowed itself to be picked up and carried to convalescence in a loose box, and Alan guilty as hell made desperate attempts to restore him to his former glory by the time the family returned.

Jolly and chatty after my brief spell away I missed my old stag's appearance and on enquiring why he was not present, Alan confessed his sins. Number two bird had by then taken over all the hens and was having a hell of a time, looking twice as big, his wattles reddening up to catch up the colours of his old rival. Sadly the old chap when recovered, never resumed his top status but quietly mooched about in his rival's shadow until the time came for him to go to market.

14

About this time I went out one morning to find a very lovely, clipped hunter without tack standing in the lane outside. Reporting it to the police, we resisted the temptation to make use of it for leisure in the same way our missing cow had been annexed by the finders. So we put it in a stable with the best of care — it was lovely to have a decent horse around again, and offered it our best hay and oats. It was several days before a groom attached to the local hunt kennels came and collected it, but alas no drink offered to the hostelry who had sheltered it!

As Philip was growing so fast we felt it would be very nice for him to have a donkey to ride, as we had some very suitable little plats (tiny paddocks) where I used to rear my goslings. We had seen an advert for a very pretty little moke, within our reach — just! Our neighbours however did not bless us for this acquisition. For some reason the sight of a donkey looking over a field gate and braying loudly seemed to have the most appalling effect on Edwin's lugubrious and gently-mannered carthorses, on several occasions seen bolting down the lane with the wagon, the old carter's legs sticking over the side, careering full gallop past our farmyard towards his stable.

To make things worse, the said donkey was then discovered to have got out in the night and wandered down the road, discovering Edwin's potato clamp, at which he helped himself liberally, narrowly missing a dangerous colic. Having reared a number of goslings, which I always found a challenge, but which made a very good price locally, the wretched moke decided to chase them around the platt and kill them by treading on them. He was then confined to the home paddock with the cows and Philip used to sit on him happily as he lay down with the herd, when he couldn't get an adult to lead him out.

The quiet rural lanes with their high earth banks provided a marvellous habitat for rabbits, and these in turn fitted into the farming business, contributing to the farm income. In the days before myxomatosis and the comparatively enormous wealth of the average urban family, the local auctioneers collated a list of farms which had a plentiful supply and were prepared to offer the rights to catch them, to the professional warreners in the area, who toured the listed farms and assessed their potential, taking into account the state of the banks and hedges for ferreting, and the acreage to be covered, putting their bids into the local auctioneer.

This was an environmentally friendly activity as of course they never removed the whole breeding colony, or their living would suffer. As a result of keeping the rabbit population in reasonable proportions we received a welcome cheque — eventually. I say eventually as the collection of this income from the band of colourful characters required some pressure. As the summer progressed it was a usual sight to see the lines of rabbits slung on poles, awaiting loading at the station, heading for the London markets — another rural activity lost in the mists of time, to the increasing wealth of city dwellers and probably to the Beeching axe on the rural railway services.

One night when we were still living in the hamlet, I was returning home from the evening milking with my bike loaded with machine units and dairy equipment, my torch picked up a pair of blazing eyes in a hole in the roadside bank. Propping the bike up I recovered a beautiful cream Polecat ferret who was very tame and rather hungry. He came home in my pocket and was lovingly tempted with feed and looked after in a broody coop. Sadly the warreners enquired if we had seen him around as he had gnawed through his line when they were digging to find him — in those days there were no radio-transcenders to make the whereabouts of terriers and ferrets easy to locate for the chaps on top. The ferret was put on a line so he could be located. I sadly had to part with him — he was a jolly little fellow.

With eighteen cows now in milk and in-calf heifers about to enter the dairy herd, we decided the time had come to install a milking parlour and it was not too difficult now we had a decent, though basic, covered concrete yard, made up with second-hand timber, the lower part of the shippon was converted into a two-unit parlour system.

As I was now heavily pregnant it was not sensible for me to be doing any more heavy work. In fact I was enormous with this child and finding life very difficult. So I retired and concentrated on domesticity. I was certainly not going into hospital with this kid — I had had a miserable time with the first one, a fast arriver in an understaffed and overcrowded Surrey National Health Hospital ward with eighteen imminent or post-parturated females and only two loos. The only hastener suggested at the time was castor oil with the sort of results easily imagined and the arrival of a ten and a half pound baby son. No, this time I intended to be in charge of events and in my own new home.

The local midwife, a sweet little person, assured us she could be with us within fifteen minutes, nevertheless, ominously, had some problems starting her car, which she left on a slight slope, 'Just in case, my dear!' This baby was so huge that I was in great distress in the last few weeks, and could scarcely breathe in bed, but I was having no truck with castor oil this time! Eventually one fine sunny June afternoon, I felt the urge to put down a decent garden path beside the front flower-beds. Getting the wheelbarrow out, I lugged some big flat Bude pebbles out from a heap in the yard, and to my satisfaction (though with some discomfort), I got them bedded down quite efficiently in the loose, dry soil.

'Making the nest,' said Alan laconically as he went past, knowing better than to try and stop me when once engaged in a project. Sure enough by evening, he asked if I wanted him to do the usual kettle-boiling routine on retiring (in case the midwife should require it — though what for I cannot imagine). 'No,' I said, — 'let's tempt the fates and see if that works.' The baby was already two weeks late. Sure enough by 12 p.m. the midwife arrived — rather late, but just in time to make the delivery of a nearly twelve pound baby-boy.

This time it was all such a happy experience. Our doctor, who came out to stitch a repair, turned on the bathroom tap, which ran as usual slightly red, and viewing the oil lamps said hastily he would arrive at 9 a.m. to tidy me up — rather a pity actually as I was jolly sore by then, but otherwise with the help of my cheery midwife friend, Alan, presiding over the household, looked after me better than any hospital nurse. Philip was genuinely thrilled to see the new arrival, and being so much senior to him was never jealous of his little brother. Getting about again in my sunny new farmhouse, with its wonderful views, was a fantastically happy time, no post-parturition blues for me. The new baby was a happy, cheery little lad, who slept peacefully all night, and was to his mother's eyes extremely handsome.

We had no money, but we had survived in an area which would today be classed as 'less favoured' and from our neighbours learned how to cope with a difficult climate, a percentage of Grade-Three soil and to enjoy to the full, the benefits of being our own masters, and the delight of children of our own.

The team preparing Leonie for a
Cleveland Bay Show, at Lea Farm

Same foal, Ramblers Larissa at the Royal Show
the following year

Book Two

15

'I called in at the solicitors today,' said Alan on his arrival home after a day devoted to trying to find solutions to his Branch members' problems, as National Farmers' Union local secretary. 'It's all going forward quite satisfactorily, we can count on going in at Michaelmas.' This was joyful news as it concerned a little rented dairy Farm near Farnham, which soon after our marriage we had tried to rent and been unable to raise capital to buy out the tenants' thirty-cow herd of pedigree Jerseys. In the intervening years the herd was down to fourteen milking cows, the tenants were moving out due to ill health. It was a lovely big house with Hop kilns attached and cowsheds and other buildings in a neat yard outside the dairy and back door.

The years immediately after leaving North Devon had not been too easy. We had had to decide whether to borrow capital and go into a bigger farm which we had seen just up the road, or with our little family move back into the fatlands of the Home Counties to try and give the boys a better start in life. With much heart-rending we sold up our herd at Hatherleigh market — a mistake as our purchaser offered a better price for it lock, stock and barrel as it turned out.

We had a farm sale of our implements etc, dead stock being the official agricultural term, curiously enough Phil's donkey, bought for £5, had stolen the whole Show. The auctioneers at first being extremely doubtful if they would have any interest at all, advised us to sell it before the sale. However news travels fast in Devon and donkeys were at that time a rarity. They were inundated with would-be buyers and as it was already sold, we had to include it and buy it back at a huge price for the lucky purchaser. The farm sale went forward with no hitches, and in due course we were once again in West Surrey, but this time Alan as Farm Manager and I as Herdswoman ensconced in a lovely Tudor house with a good set of dairy buildings where we built up yet another pedigree Guernsey herd for our employer, a business man living some distance away.

Philip, seven years, by then went to prep school in Cranleigh, cycling down the estate drive in the morning, leaving his cycle at the lodge and walking to the bus stop half a mile away, to travel the four miles to Cranleigh, where he walked the rest of the way to school, returning the same way at night. As he passed a flower shop in the bus, on my birthday he walked another half mile to the shop and bought me a plant for my garden, catching the bus just in time to come home. Life was very different then!

In due course our employer decided to build a new house for himself on the farm, and left the delights of suburban Byfleet for the fastnesses of the Surrey Hills. As his eldest daughter, still at school, wanted to keep a horse, once again I was able to get some pleasant riding in a new and very picturesque setting, for a stabled horse needs daily exercise. Our Guernsey herd went from strength to strength and though we only employed one general farm worker on the hundred and fifty acre farm we also made use of Smithwood common which had been ploughed in wartime and had now fallen back into rough grass. This we cut for hay as the herd numbered eventually some fifty head.

Alan and I and our sons were so very happy here, the only trouble being that our employers were not so happy having moved out of their sociable urban existence into a totally isolated environment. I think the happy life of their workers irritated our employers who walked about like Mr and Mrs Glum, and just as we had the herd up to a really high standard we were told that they had decided to sell up. This was sad news for us, as it meant us giving up our lovely Tudor home. Our herd sale was a great success but it all seemed such a waste of time and effort and we were not anxious to face this sort of situation in the future whenever we had put our roots down. 'Just as one door shuts, another slams,' as one of our jolly AG. reps used to say about life.

We were in borrowed cottages before Alan was offered an Assistant County Secretary's post in the National Farmers' Union, The senior man was on the verge of retirement and was training up staff to take his place. This job was exactly what Alan wanted and in the Guildford area which embraced the adjoining areas of Chiddingfold, Hambledon and Farnham. He already knew this area particularly well having been educated at Cranleigh School, and received a basic salary for all the NFU services, very many in those days, as it was a wonderful service for the smaller farmer, and also had insurance income from his own insurance groups. It was a large area and he and his partner David after the retirement of their boss, split the management of the smaller branches between them, David taking on Guildford and Dorking, and the market Garden Business —

very substantial in north east Surrey, Alan — Chiddingfold, Hambledon and Farnham.

During this early apprenticeship to the NFU one of our kind farmer friends had offered us a disused farm cottage. With it was a semi-detached older derelict cottage. This was in a really isolated spot next to his outlying farm buildings, and approached down a narrow unmade lane. We agreed to keep an eye on his sheep and other stock, and he allowed us to do up the adjacent cottage as extra playrooms for the boys. It was great fun and of course all done in Alan's spare time on a shoe string. As the old cottage had a brick floor Alan came home with a wonderful find. One of his grower clients presented us with yards and yards of very heavy quality jute matting coloured green, which he was given every year after the Motor Show to screen his plants from frost and high winds. With this very wide matting we covered all the ground floors — the stairs being knocked down at a previous date when the cottage was used for farm storage.

Neither cottage had main electricity, we used Calor gas for lighting and cooking, but we did have main water this time. Keeping a watching brief on Lewis' sheep meant braving a very large and sassy Dorset Horn ram. The ewes which lambed twice a year were one of the largest breeds of sheep in the country and they had to be kept on a high plane of nutrition to achieve two lamb crops. I am not a good counter, in fact I had a good deal of sympathy with the German guards who had difficulty counting our prisoners of war, as I seemed to have no confidence in any total I came up with, indeed counting sheep to get to sleep induced only nightmares.

During the counting process the ram was clever in working his way behind one, and it was his goal to charge one from the rear of the knee joints. I managed to avoid this myself, but coming upon Lewis after breakfast one day I managed to get grudging agreement that the ram was a 'proper bastard', he having fallen victim to one of his rear attacks. Farming has never been an easy way of life, and on one particularly bleak winter's morning Lewis's comment on his morning rounds of a large mixed farm, had a ring of sincerity I have never forgotten. 'Good morning. Hah! Terrible day, everything dead or dying.'

Only stock-farmers would feel affinity for the above statement in a bad spell of weather. Lewis kept a large amiable shire mare at our yard which was used for all the odd jobs. She had a nice large paddock at the back of our house, on a wooded sandy slope. In a spell of suitable weather, I approached our landlord about the possibility of my being able to keep a riding horse in his field and was delighted when he agreed.

On one of our first holidays in the New Forest with the family, I found an upstanding New Forest cross thoroughbred three-year-old gelding belonging to a Commoner (a New Forest farmer with forest rights). He was kind enough to allow us to watch the 'colt-hunters' running the Forest-bred mares and their foals into the 'Drift' — gated at both ends, the foals to be branded with their owner's individual brand, mares' tails to have a few hairs cut in a distinct way by the agisters in charge of Forest affairs so that they could be identified as having paid the 'tail' charge for the current season.

Our little family really loved this time-old operation. The wild herds galloping in with tremendous flourish, nostrils wide, manes and tails flying. The Commoner owners on their fast well-trained mounts, cracking their whips to see the ponies did not cut back to the wild, and when safely shut in back again to the open Forest to collect more stragglers. What was so interesting to us was to see how placid the ponies became when incarcerated. Heads dropped, resting a leg or picking over the grass within the large enclosure placidly, were the foals, yearlings and growing two and three year olds. Only the two or three stallions loudly proclaiming their rights over their own band.

These scenes made an indelible memory for the whole family. The visit to Beaulieu Road Sale Ring, set in the middle of the heather-clad heath and made of natural local materials by the Commoners' Defence Association for the sale of their Forest-bred stock. A glorious chance for anyone with an eye for a pony to find a foal or yearling for a few pounds, as rearing was expensive for their breeders, only the really strong, fit ponies surviving the rugged upbringing. We have picked out numbers of lovely ponies from these rough sales, which have become first-class performers and on one occasion a mare who was champion at the National Pony Society's Show at Malvern the following August.

It is a way of life which has not altered too much since the days of Henry the Eighth who was responsible for some special regulations regarding the running of stock on the Royal hunting grounds of the New Forest (new at the time of William the Conqueror). One of these, now consistently overlooked, was that Commoners' rights could only extend to the number of animals depastured, on the Forest, that their Forest holdings could enclose at home. So that if all stock was ordered off the Forest by the Monarch, either for his pleasure in the case of hunting the Royal deer, or by other necessity, these animals might be kept away from Forest grazing until allowed back.

Many of the Forest holdings were merely a cottage and paddock in which a cow and pigs were probably stalled as well, so that the numbers of ponies on the Forest were regulated and so avoided overgrazing the 'lawns' as the best grazing is called. Another interesting fact was that with constant threat of war, Henry the Eighth decreed that all stallions turned out on the Forest must exceed fourteen hands so that there was always a ready stock of sturdy mounts growing on for war requirements. All stallions had to be inspected (as they are to this day) and those not up to standard, had to be slaughtered and buried in the Forest. Nowadays all stallions must be under 14.2 hands.

In our early years in the New Forest, the ponies had the right to come right into the villages, and in the summer when the flies were trying they would 'shade' from early morning to evening in the main street of Lyndhurst and Brockenhurst. To the many visitors the sight of the little foals laid asleep outside the shop doors beside their dams was absolutely fascinating — not so the shopkeepers, who had to take a broom and shovel out during the day, to clean up the pavements and try to repel the flies the ponies brought in with them.

Unfortunately when my new purchase came home, we found a nasty little wound behind the girth under the belly, which must have happened during the round-up when he came off the Forest. I of course mentioned this to the vendor and he said to see how it went on. I was able to start breaking him in and found him a sweet and amenable youngster. However as time went on Beaulieu Boy as we called him, who carried our little sons about very kindly, did not appear to be recovering from this deep wound although he did not seem to have any pain and put on condition and bloomed.

Taking up my horsy neighbour's offer I presented him to an equine specialist who was visiting their racehorses. His examination brought a worried frown to his expression, with misgivings about a fistular which could cause all sorts of internal problems and his suggestion as to whether we could return him to the vendor. We were quite unworried about this as the breeder was a very esteemed local farmer whose word was as good as his bond. He had no other large pony he could replace him with, but offered us two little black fillies of his breeding aged three years which were persistently getting into Lymington and thence into the public pound, an expensive exercise. He warned us that they might be in foal to a Forest stallion. Because of their liking for holiday makers and the delights of town life, they were incredibly easy to break in. Beaulieu Boy eventually recovered from his wound and was ridden by his breeder who was suitably pleased by his initial training with us and was his preferred choice as a colt-hunting ride.

Lewis was interested in our deal with the Forest ponies but was firm that he had agreed that I should have one horse not two. It was quite easy for us to find a nice home for the larger of the two black fillies who was the oldest, as she was by then very quiet to ride and in fact our purchasers came at night and bought her by the head lamps of their car. The remaining pony we registered with the New Forest Society as Sherbet; she was definitely in foal and quiet enough for George who was now three and a half years old to ride on a leading rein and in fact during the winter I used to lead them both all over Newlands Corner, when hounds were about; as we cut cross country we were never far from the action.

The following spring the grass was very poor. I felt she really must have better keep if she was to get any milk. We managed to find her some lovely grazing on river meadows grazed by cattle. Borrowing a trailer we took her by road the four miles to her new home. Within forty-eight hours of arrival she disappeared. Desperately worried as to where she could have gone as the cattle were all safe and the adjoining roads heavily trafficked, when at last I was fearing she had been stolen or fallen in the river, I had a phone call from our neighbours: 'Sonia, your little mare was waiting at the bridleway gate to be let through. I have opened it and sent her down to you.'

How Sherbet found her way home cross country through woods and tracks unknown to her and unobserved by urban dog walkers we shall never know. Within a fortnight she had foaled a big black filly which loved lying around in the sun. As the mare had a huge milk supply despite the lack of grass, we called the filly Rambler's Siesta, and as a strapping two year old with mother's marvellous temperament, she was sent off to her new home in Sussex on her own in a railway horsebox ordered up for our use by

Southern Railway for loading at Chilworth station.

For the next seven years we heard no more about her, so when we saw her advertised in *Horse and Hound* as a ten-year-old ex-junior show jumper in foal with her first baby, I couldn't wait to get her home. She had been jumped up to Junior Grade A standard, winning at Hickstead, with Malory Spens who had gone up to senior grades. On arrival Siesta was very quiet in her stable, taking in the change of scenery. She gave no sign of recognising me for the first two days — then showing some friends around the stud, we passed her box and laughed at a cheeky foal in the next paddock. As soon as she heard my laugh, the years rolled back and she neighed incessantly for ten minutes showing a real delight to be with us. Her first foal was a colt and was sold.

Her second foal by Pickwick we named Rambler's Selena, and as a yearling she was first at Windsor and also at the Surrey County. By the time we took her to the Breed Show at Burley in the New Forest, we had a lot of interest in her from German breeders who were waiting to see their judgement confirmed by the judge, so it was very fortunate that in fact she won there too and they confirmed their purchase as she came

189

out of the ring. Later in these recollections I will describe use we made of this sale in setting up our own beef herd. Selena's dam, Siesta, went to Holland to some Dutch clients of ours, and took another child through the junior jumping ratings before she finally retired.

16

The 1960s were not particularly affluent years as the country struggled out of post-war shortages. I managed to do some part-time jobs to help support the family, and it was whilst dog walking for the Kennels at Farley-Green that walking over the heath I spotted a dear little cottage which was apparently empty (the previous tenant's bed having dropped through the floor into the sitting room) belonging to Albury Park. Work having been completed, the estate were deciding whether to sell it. There were two little paddocks beside it and about 13,000 acres of forestry and common lands all round it so the out-riding was superb.

This really had our name on it and having bought it we enjoyed doing the cottage up and building our little stable yard. The two paddocks were overgrown with weeds to the height of Alan's shoulders so we started off by hiring an Alan scythe.

The day was warm, the land on a slope, and after an hour or so of tiny progress, my good husband looked red-faced-on the verge of a seizure. After a stop for a hot drink we both said, 'This needs Foresters.' After a visit to the sales we had six unbroken ponies to start the clearance project.

As we had not yet moved in, I thought it strange that only five could be seen as I came down the lane every day to feed them hay and yet by the time I parked at the cottage the sixth always appeared. Later when a new-comer to the village turned a mare in their paddock half a mile away, there were definitely only five in our fields. On investigation I found that in the Forestry adjoining our boundary fence of five strands of taut barbed wire, a pony had obviously established his 'haunt', over many weeks, and eschewing his grazing duties on our property, jumped the five foot fence twice a day. The arrival of the new mare at the other end of the Forestry in a post and rail enclosure was much easier to surmount to share her rations. Spartan made a wonderful showjumper but his new owners — a riding school — never knew which paddock to collect him from.

We called our little cottage Rambler's, because of the roses, and immediately registered the same name as our prefix with the New Forest Society and later in the central prefix Register as soon as it came on the scene in the late '70s, because sometimes clients were inclined to add our own prefix on to animals they had themselves bred which was very confusing. However in these early days, the New Forest Society was just emerging from the umbrella of the National Pony Society to form their own *Stud Book*, so it was a good time for us to set up a stud of our own.

Alan was asked if he would take on the secretaryship of the Chiddingfold Farmers' Foxhounds — his happy relationship with most of the farmers in the hunt country was obviously a boon for the Committee, and from that time the whole family enjoyed nine seasons of wonderful fun and great sport. Bob Buswell was our huntsman in the early years, a happier hunt would have been impossible to find, as this wartime pack was started in 1941 to control a plague of foxes which had invaded the area, after hunting shut down at the outbreak of war. It was truly a farmers' pack, and in every way needed by the landowners and farmers of West Surrey.

I was 'Joint' so on Wednesdays had to cope with collecting 'caps' (contributions paid by visitors on a short-term basis, and tradition-ally collected in a hunting cap), and also of course welcoming subscribers, landowners and farmers as well as the army of country helpers who are the lifeblood of a successful hunt, many of whom had an encyclopaedic knowledge of the terrain and mounted on bicycles or in cars, quietly parked up in an inconspicuous place could be relied upon to give reliable information to pass on to master or huntsman.

The Pony Club Branch was an integral part of the hunt, and we had some very keen children out hunting — Bob showing the most effective riders how to whip in to hounds, which entailed knowing all the hounds' names, and thus encouraging them to go off on their own to collect any stray hounds and bring them back to the pack — albeit under covert supervision from Committee members present at the children's meet.

Little Rambler's with its apron of mown grass common outside the gate was a favourite meet when a human 'fox' had to provide sport over the common and ponies were left in their stables in snowy school holidays. After providing hospitality for numerous children after the meet, there was a rush to find their Jodh boots as they got to the back door where wintry draughts were stealing in, and dozens of pairs of identical boots were scattered around for them to try and identify.

The Chid. Farmers' Pony Club's ideal was that with a percentage of town children on hired or borrowed mounts, they must never receive less attention than the luckier children with expensive competition ponies who were likely to progress to prestigious Branch teams. The former were less easy to teach and really needed enthusiastic support to show them how to improve their riding and their pony to mutual advantage — it was often just this extra interest from their instructor that decided them to try and retrain their ponies or possibly their parents to try and find them a more suitable mount, so they could have more fun.

There is an enormous amount of work carried out by so many people in Pony Club activities, and although we had some really generous landowners who offered their land, swimming pools, stable yards etc to the Pony Club, also two dedicated Branch instructors, one person who will always stand out in my memory was Una Mizen, wife of the Hunt Chairman, who not only instructed but stored the club jumps and transported them to all activities, where if she was lucky some help was given her to put them up — however like any other hunt activity, at the end of the day, whether point-to-point organisation — hunter trials or Pony Club rallies, loading up the 'props' after the event, when you have been on duty all day and your back is breaking, sorts out the men from the boys, and all too many sporting enthusiasts manage to evade this onerous duty with excuses about feeding the horses left at home. It can be a lonely and defeating job on your own, or with insufficient help, those who carry out these selfless tasks are to my mind absolute martyrs.

Eventually our little cottage was sold and the time came for moving into the new dairy farm. It was also so typical that at the last minute our sale fell through. Of course we had to move out and take up our tenancy, together with the pedigree Jersey herd from the outgoing tenant. Fortunately some farming friends of ours added these quality milkers to their own herd, so that at least went smoothly, but how I hated leaving our little cottage empty, in its isolated position, especially as it was a particularly cold autumn.

Fortunately friends of ours bought Rambler's and whilst the solicitors were as usual making a meal of the totally straightforward conveyancing, our friends asked if they could go in and 'look after' the plumbing, in case it should freeze up.

Naturally the solicitors had a fit, and said no one should go in until contract exchange, but being trustful idiots we were quite happy for them to do so, and they were able to light the Rayburn and keep the cottage dry until they completed the sale. As our friends' husband was a sick man, we always felt that this lovely home in the Surrey Hills gave him an extra lease in life, as they loved living there, as we had done, and stayed many years.

17

Lickfolds Farm was in the heart of the village of Rowledge — close to the Hampshire border. Philip was by then going to Lingfield Secondary Modern School, which ran a farming course alongside the normal curriculum; this meant he was a week-day boarder, living in digs in the village with a friendly widow lady, and returning on the train to Farnham on Saturday night. George was accepted as a day-boy at Frensham Heights School which was a half-mile walk from the farm. Later on we were able to rent their surplus parkland and keep our cattle and horses there.

One of our earliest outings was to go down to Wimborne and see a New Forest colt foal, which was to become our stud stallion. He was impeccably bred from a very successful stud owned by Mrs Haycock. Peveril Pickwick was a very large black colt with very good bone. (He eventually grew nine inches of bone below the knee, equivalent to a good hunter.) He had been seen by many breeders who at that time were unused at seeing the larger type of Forest pony. He was not yet weaned and had been given a marvellous start by his dam. We agreed to buy him for one hundred pounds, and he proved to be one of the best investments we ever made. When he came home Alan had just finished making him a large cage box in our hop-kiln. He lived opposite our fourteen-hand New Forest mare, Rambler's Isobelle, who had carried my vast weight of thirteen stone, effortlessly, and was quiet enough for George to ride out hunting. We had to cobble up some boxes for our two hunters. Whilst Alan was at work, his office now at Milford, I had an incredibly difficult job to keep water running in this fairly exposed position on the hills above Farnham.

Moving is a very stressful business, and I did not realise until many months afterwards, that I had contracted me what we called 'Yuppie flu' at that time. This made everything a much greater struggle and it was nearly twelve months before I felt myself again. We had a fairly long drive to hunt with the 'Farmers' but to the surprise of the Committee we were punctual as usual for our duties. Punctuality is an attitude of mind, and Alan and I can always get to any function after the longest drive on time, as indeed can most hunting and showing folk. It never fails to amaze me that wherever a meet is held in the quietest of country, within ten minutes of 11 a.m. large numbers of lorries and trailers quietly arrive, or if no parking, an orderly quiet stream of mounted followers appear as if by magic, to be quietly present as master, huntsman and hounds arrive.

In due course the structural alterations agreed with our landlord's agent were completed. Alan by now an expert in getting hold of second-hand building timber — which in an area of former Army camps, now coming into civilian use, was in the hands of the gypsy demolition families.

Apart from our two hunters we also had several sweet New Forest fillies to breed with Pickwick when he was older. We entered him for all the top New Forest shows as a yearling, but he never got to any of them, having grown disjointedly either up on his rump or high on the withers — falling off at the tail, just as he was due to appear. He was two years old before Alan started him on his show career — and please note, any ladies who bemoan their husbands are not interested in their pony-showing hobby, certain sacrifices on your own part have to be made — men like to win. Your best prospect must be made over to them, and a good deal of preparation and training behind the scenes to ensure initial placing is possible — then with a little success they're hooked!

Pickwick and Alan once started at an early Hickstead mixed-breed class, worked his way steadily through the salad (yellow and green rosettes) to the coveted reds and blues. Within a year or two we knew we were on to something as our main opposition in the stallion classes were two virtually unbeatable ponies. (One's opposition are always the best Judges). When their positions appeared threatened their owners sold them overseas, and Pickwick reigned supreme for many, many years, eventually becoming the first New Forest stallion to qualify for the Horse of the Year Show at Wembley.

Our original blue diesel land rover and Rice three-horse trailer (both bought brand new for nine hundred pounds total — collecting the trailer from Leicester where it was adjusted to the hitch) — a luxury we have never managed since, had done good service, but as we were now travelling further for our hunting, and showing at the Royal and National Pony Society at Malvern, collecting and delivering stud visitors and delivering home-bred stock, we felt we had better find a lorry, and as at that time the name Bedford T K was synonymous with reliability, we fell for one offered us by a fellow hunting acquaintance. As he parted with it his last words were: 'I would be happy to sell this to my best friend.' These were famous last words, as it happened to turn out; it seemed we used the same mechanic. When our new lorry was playing up and we took it down to him to look over, we were dashed to hear him say, 'I am afraid you've bought a dud there. I advised him to get rid of it as soon as possible, as I am not prepared to spend any more time on it.' Naturally Alan was not prepared to accept this state of affairs as we had paid a decent price for it. By the farmers' network the original tribal drums, we managed to find an engineer who worked for a large haulage firm, all using Bedfords.

Dear Graham, how much we owe him. Not only did he take over our new purchase, and for a nominal sum get it up to scratch, but he also looked after our lorry for many years and taught Alan to take down and maintain a Bedford Diesel, and to get it through the MOT annually. We did tremendous mileages in that lorry, which we kept for many years. It even travelled to France on two occasions ending up at the Swiss border when we delivered our New Forest ponies abroad. It also ran up to Wetherby sales with not less than three young Cleveland crosses every year as well as all our showing and stud transport.

Later on it carried cattle and pedigree bulls

as well, and whenever we saw our lorry's vendor we delightedly told him how grateful we were that he had supplied us such a marvellous vehicle! In the end he forgot to look sick and convinced himself he had done us a favour.

Once we had got settled into Lickfolds, I was able to start a project I had in mind for many years: this was to breed Cleveland Bay horses, a rare breed originating in Yorkshire, a photograph of which I had in my post-war agricultural reference books on British livestock and horses. I thought they looked a marvellous type of horse to make a heavy hunter. I have never changed my mind in the following fifty years — also in this book were illustrations of Belted Galloway cattle another dream which took many years to fulfil.

Cleveland Bays are not only a rare breed but are also on the very endangered rare breed list; originally bred by most of the Yorkshire Dale farmers for general work on the land and also widely used by the travelling 'Chapmen', travelling in convoys over the North Yorkshire Moors to deliver panniered goods to the isolated communities before the roads were suitable for wheeled traffic. Captain Fairfax Blakeborough who was for many years a correspondent of the *Racing Post* while he was Breed Secretary of the Cleveland Bay Society researched the early annals of *Racing in the North* and discovered that the blood of some of the early racehorses lies at the roots of the Cleveland Bay ancestry. This was after the importation of the Barbe horses, when racehorses were run in several heats on one day, so that staying-blood was essential.

When at last the roads got better they were used as carriage horses as well as work on the land, and at the zenith of the coaching and for high-class carriage work in London, a separate section of the *Cleveland Bay Stud Book* was called the Yorkshire Coach Horse Society, the progeny of Cleveland to the English thoroughbred producing the really flashy driving horses required for the smart London trade. These lovely horses were walked down to the London markets. Between the First and Second World War, it is not generally known that over thirty Cleveland Bay stallions were exported to Germany for the improvement of their many excellent generic breeds.

It is I am afraid rather typical of Britain that stock of foreign sources is seen as more valuable than those native to Britain. Of course this also applies to British farmers buying into European beef breeds, whilst the Germans were wisely picking out our finest

Aberdeen Angus or others, Hereford beef stock.

However to return to the Clevelands during the First World War, enormous numbers of these horses were taken by the Army. Very active clean-legged horses (without hairy heels) were suitable for the highly mobile gun teams. During this period the Cleveland blood lines were flexible enough to go back to the earlier smaller Chapman-type horses for war service. Throughout the early nineteenth century the USA were keen buyers of this breed, and in fact some astute young Yorkshire men immigrated and established a big demand there for their native breed. However after the Second World War when a tally was taken, there were only nine pure-bred mares registered in Great Britain, and it took several decades and some grading-up (under supervision) to get the numbers of pure-breds up to even the small number of forty or so foals registered annually today.

It was hardly surprising that we should find buying into this breed very difficult. Eventually two filly-foals bred by Lady Hudson, at her estate in Westbury, Wiltshire came into the market. They were to be sold at the Yorkshire horse sales of J Stephenson (long-time secretary of the breed); their breeder particularly wished to give the society her support. Philip and I journeyed down to see them; the whole family turned out in the field together. We were given two bags of lump sugar and told by the farm staff to get on with it! The sugar was obviously to keep the stallion occupied whilst we looked at the other four. However we headed for the gate when he finished the sugar as he had obviously been rather spoiled by the farm staff.

There was always considerable interest in Stephenson's CB Section of the sales and there were always some very nice first-cross hunters bred from the many good thoroughbred stallions in that area; a lot of this stock went show jumping. The Yorkshire CB breeders welcomed interest from the South, but though we had to pay a lot of money by northern standards for our filly, there was at that time considerable difference in values from north and south. It was a long drive in our lorry but the roads were very quiet in those days. When the motorway opened for some time none would use it so in our many trips up and down to Yorkshire the trip was not as bad as it is today.

Manningford Iris, our new foal, was a strong, good looking filly, sturdy as a young oak, with a kind and sensible temperament.

No doubt the many Cleveland enthusiasts helping with the sale, had educated her on the ground before the sale. Quite unworried by the four-hundred mile round trip, she was quite happy to grow up with the native pony stock, and as we envisaged breeding from her, we decided to look out for a decent colt, one with equable temperament and suitable for riding so that if we could not find any local interest in using him for producing weight-carriers, he could always be gelded and carry Alan to hounds.

In due course we were told of a nice four year old which had been leased to a northern breeder for the previous season and we travelled up to inspect a group of really lovely pure-breds he had sired — running with their dams on high ground above the North Sea. It was a bleak farm to the eye of a southerner. The mares lived out all winter and each received a stook (no combines at that time) of unthreshed oats per day. The farmer told me that his cows had to wait until June 1st for an 'early bite'. It was a tragedy that most of these foals were dead the following spring, despite entreaties of local farmers to accept some extra feed for them.

Travelling some distance to the outskirts of a smoky industrial city we found the driving-horse stables, where the colt was stabled with his full-brother, which, being sired by HM The Queen's stallion, Mulgrave Supreme, was being retained by his owner. We liked him enough to venture four hundred pounds on him — a large sum in those days; he was unbroken and we got him home as quickly as possible. Pickwick was moved out of his oast house palace into other accommodation, and with Knaresborough Sir Robert now at home with us, and the stud season over the horizon, we thought we had better introduce him to a possible clientele.

Accordingly invitation cards were sent to all our hunting and showing friends for an *at home* with Sir Robert. As the oast house was integral to our living quarters, Robert thoroughly enjoyed visitors coming in to him glasses and sandwiches in hand all evening. It was all very informal and everyone was impressed by his amiable temperament and of course with his huge bone and majestic bearing. He was a wow. The following season we had some thirty mares visiting, on his first season in the south.

Now we had two stallions and a number of hunters and ponies about the place we decided to look for a student who would like to live in with us, en-famille, and learn to keep our youngstock to show standard, and help us with all the stud duties. Janet came to us aged sixteen, having had some excellent experience at Valerie Millwood's showing stables. With a great sense of humour and tough enough to tackle any job, she soon became one of the family. Her first assignment was to take Isobelle who I had been using on Wednesdays to collect caps — my usual mount recovering from a severe attack of equine flu, and who was subsequently very fit — in for the first Silver Horseshoe thirty-mile ride organised by the New Forest Society. I had intended to do this myself but an attack of piles made this impossible, so Janet, a lightweight, was allocated this place.

Alan and I groomed for her at the various vet and rest gates. She was extremely conscientious and timed her arrival at these points meticulously, as we emphasised that she should aim to go through absolutely calm and collected. In fact we discovered later that in a rush of rather overexcited, impetuous riders she had found one other girl who had the same ideas, and when the ponies heated up, they rubbed them down with bracken just out of sight of the vet points and rode quietly through together.

They were allowed an eight mph speed required for the ride which concluded at Janesmoor Pond. At which point they were given a fifteen-minute respite before riding a small show for the judges. As Alan got Janet out of the saddle, wiped her boots clean and fed and watered her, I did the same for Is, who was enjoying herself immensely and cooling off in the pond, was tucking into some 'goodies' herself. I was very proud to see my prodigies going so well in the show ring, and Janet was absolutely thrilled to receive the Silver Horseshoe so soon after arriving with us.

Alan with Peveril Pickwick, winner at
Hickstead Mountain and Moorland Classes
at two years of age

Peveril Pickwick as champion

18

There was an awful lot to do at Lickfolds to make it suitable for our purposes. Eventually the landlord offered to sell it to us at sitting-tenant value. As we had no manege or suitable enclosure for breaking a big stallion, we decided to let our friend, Brian Crago, have him for a couple of weeks to break him to saddle in his lovely indoor school close by. We had very good reports of his progress so he was home within a fortnight ready for my initial ride on him. I got on him at the mounting block outside the hop kiln and Alan accompanied me through the yard and into a large level field we called the 'Airfield'. Robert was interested and delighted in this fascinating course of events and obviously remembered his activities in the Yorkshire Dales. Whilst perfectly balanced on the bit, in the middle of the field, he let off an enormous volley of bucks with sheer delight at being ridden out of doors for the first time.

I was very glad to have long legs and also to have had the foresight to have lengthened my stirrups, so I managed to avoid falling off, and rode him through this boisterous outburst, after which, he never ever gave me any trouble again, save one bitterly cold day when at the Cleveland Bay stallion Show on Wetherby racecourse, I was exercising him in the roughs before taking him into the ring before a hastily planned ridden parade, when in the middle of a strong canter, he spotted a pen of laying hens and a cockerel hovering up on the horizon, a combination which was too tempting to miss, after many hours in a horsebox.

Pickwick was also backed by us at home, and by that time we had NPS stud students as we were a certified stud training centre; we usually had a lightweight around who was delighted to hack him out. However we have always felt that to make clever stallions who have the ability to face up to bossy, dangerous mares, or spend hours wooing a nervous filly, it is much better to concentrate on their real job in life which is to dominate and not be subject to the onerous disciplines of a continual competitive nature, which is the sphere of geldings or non-breeding mares.

However as we were campaigning our Cleveland stallion as a first rate outcross for the thoroughbred mare, to get hunters and show jumpers, I managed to get a few days hunting in a suitable part of our hunt country, on Robert who could be seen to be a mannered and active participant. Lickfolds Farm, unlike Rambler's which was situated on Surrey's sandy heaths, was on a heavy loam soil. By midwinter the tracks through the back yards were stiff with mud which could remove your boot — particularly difficult when collecting and turning out young horses. During the Easter hols, Alan and the boys had a really good session one weekend and got a concrete mixer in and put down hardcore and concrete which was a wonderful boon.

It was then that Phil starting up our tractor, swung the starting handle when the Massey Ferguson was in gear. By the Grace of God he managed to avoid being run over, but the tractor proceeded on its way in our ancient implement shed, constructed of corrugated iron upon wooden poles, knocking out two roof supports, a shattered Philip having to report the damages to his dad. This seemed a good chance to replace the building with a decent-sized wide-span concrete building, which would also serve as a manege, albeit half-sized sixty by forty feet. So after the Planning Office had been satisfied that it was a replacement, we then fixed with a well-known firm of pre-fab concrete buildings to undertake this work in the spring when the land was drier.

Railway ballast makes a marvellous hard-standing and once Alan had cleared away the tin, the Southern Railways ballast dump a mile away supplied a really ample base for the new building — which, it must be confessed, was rather larger than the original. On the set day in early spring, Alan and I awaited the arrival of the erection gang. First of all came two enormous mobile cranes which hung over our farm, warning our neighbours that immediate action would probably be necessary to prevent the erection of what threatened to be a twelve-storey building, this of course was most unsuitably brought to us on a Friday ready for a Monday start. Following the cranes were four lorry loads of concrete stanchions, roofing etc, and an artic lorry with forty-foot long beams. These pulled up in single file through our field access and ground to a stop as by then the erection foreman considered the land too soft to take the two Cranes into their working position. As there was no further room for any vehicle to move in or out of the yard the drivers one and all repaired to the Hare and Hounds pub to await further instructions from Kent.

It was then my wonderful husband came into his own; displaying managerial skills and personal magnetism, he rushed down to the

Railway ballast yard and found an owner-driver who agreed to come at once. With manly leadership, and comradely drive, he rushed into the pub and extracted the drivers by telling them their lorries were sinking — strong words being necessary to get some action, and then with some difficulty, backing and shuffling lorries got the ballast tipping lorry ahead of the queue, to make a base to get the cranes up to the site. With these the concrete beams were unloaded and swung clear of the existing buildings, ready for Monday erection, and the queue of lorries returned to Kent. All weekend we soothed hysterical but normally most cooperative neighbours assuring them that they would not know the building was there after the cranes had gone.

Another of Alan's creations was a four-box stallion yard with a clock tower and weather vane over the main entrance. I was absolutely thrilled with this unit, constructed out of ex-military timber at a minimal cost. Truly to be well-endowed financially would be a boon, but not necessarily guaranteeing happy relations — whilst a clever, innovative husband who enjoys making things for his wife's business, is a jewel in the crown for any happily married woman.

About this time Philip who although

trained to manage intensive poultry units, after attending Plumpton Agricultural College, found this dusty indoor occupation not entirely to his liking or good for his health. After calf rearing in some rented buildings he was taken on by Mrs Bill Powell at Lingfield to help her with the thoroughbred Hunters Improvement stallions (The Stud Book Society prior to the present British Sports Horse Society), a stud which her husband had run so successfully for many years. Philip loved this job, and at this time the four or five stallions attracted enormous interest from southern breeders. Employing a young staff, with a head-girl who had worked with her husband, Phil and one other girl, they had the responsibility for hundreds of mares during the season and thus Phil got more experience there than we could give him at home.

A Sussex Cleveland Bay breeder sent his stud manager with mares to be covered by the Premium stallions, and during this visit the stud man unburdened himself to Phil about the Clevelands which he found too large for comfort; he was putting pressure on his boss to change them for flat-racing types. It was not long after this that I had a call from the owner of the two pure-bred mares, their foals, and the now gelded stallion which he was driving. The price of this consignment was not overly large but when we went over with the lorry to fetch them home my hand trembled as never before when writing out such a large cheque — only possible by my successful overtures to my bank manager for an overdraft (those were the days.)

As Iris was now in foal to Sir Robert, we now had three Cleveland brood mares and a classy driving gelding, so when I saw in the *Breed Newsletter*, that both the Royal Mews and the Japanese Royal family were looking for suitable stock I pricked up my ears and got on the phone — obviously first to the Royal Mews who needed a matched pair of Cleveland driving horses for the wedding parade of HRH Princess Anne. In due course Arthur Showell, head coachman to HM The Queen at that time, came down to see Zephyr who was not much over sixteen hands high. No decisions could be made until a matching pair could be found, but I was told they really required rather bigger horses as some of the ceremonial coaches were very heavy. However Arthur Showell was a most interesting raconteur with a depth of experience in driving coaching teams in the private sector, prior to joining the Royal Mews.

Whilst we were awaiting the decisions of the Mews, our youngest student rode Zephyr all over the district, beside our other stallions, so we had a chance to see, demonstrated, the kind character of the sire of one of our newly acquired foals, out of Cholderton Quickthorn, which we registered as Rambler's Windbreak, the foundation mare of our famous Rambler's Lee family.

In due course after several months of debate, a larger pair of driving horses were found in Yorkshire for the Mews, and so I quickly wrote to the Imperial stud in Japan where I knew the standard of horse-keeping was every bit as high as in our own country. An immediate reply came back that they wished to buy Zephyr, who was by the same sire as Iris our young brood mare and one other brood mare. Obviously it was rather necessary for me to deal with the bank overdraft with dispatch, and so a substantial figure was agreed for Iris and Zephyr to go out to Japan and join the Cleveland Bays at the Imperial stud on the hills well above Tokyo's pollution problems. Their Clevelands were also used for ceremonial purposes and I hoped that they would keep us informed as to their progress. A large jet plane of the Japanese Royal Flight was sent to collect them, so they had an easy journey to their new home.

We continued to collect Clevelands whenever we could, and when my old family friends, Bob and Olive Dymond, passed away, to my surprise they had left me a little legacy. This windfall allowed me to purchase a very well-bred filly-foal from one of our stud clients, Mr and Mrs Sinclair, who had several nice Cleveland Bay mares. As my dear sailing friends had a little motor-boat called the Bolive — which at the time of Dunkirk in 1940 made repeated trips under fire to rescue our troops from the beaches and survived to go back on her moorings at Topsham on the River Exe, I called the filly Bolivia in remembrance. She subsequently bred numbers of beautiful foals for us and one year at the Royal Show was breed-champion, her two-year-old daughter who accompanied her, was reserve champion and her foal at foot, was first in her class. That was a long day, in very hot weather. I was only just over a severe leg operation and poor Alan had to find some help, to get the trio led in the Grand Parade, whilst I lay in the shade of the temporary stables, with a nasty attack of heat exhaustion, wrists in buckets of water and wet stable-rubbers over my face and feet. Eventually the Sinclairs sold us their remaining Clevelands because they knew we would treasure them.

Belties in the park

Dogs awaiting orders

19

Ruth Kitchen, the doyenne of the Northern Breeders, resided at Fryup Gill near Whitby. After the war when Cleveland numbers were very few indeed her enthusiasm helped the breed to get on its feet again. In her little bungalow surrounded by the most precipitous fields, enthusiasts for the breed from all over the country found their way to her door, always sure of a genuine welcome. As a retired legal-eagle on one occasion she travelled down to London to support the Secretariat in their application for a grant from the Racecourse Betting Levy Board. She kept and bred from a small band of mares, solicitously watched over as she grew older by her neighbour from America House, Jack Welford — always known as 'America' Jack to identify him from the numerous Jacks and other members of the Welford family also breeding Clevelands.

Ruth gave us great encouragement from the first telling me to keep an eye on Fisherman, bred by herself in case he ever came up for sale. Like most Yorkshire breeders at that time, she was apt to be vague at the boundaries of the Southern Counties and Fisherman who was supposed to be residing 'near you' turned out to be in Devon, hunting with the Axe Vale. However that was near enough for us to make contact with his owner and go and see him. He was by then ten years of age, and had been hunted several seasons having very few mares to visit at stud. During this time he had accumulated some blemishes including a big knee on one leg, and tendon trouble on the other.

Poor old chap he looked very down on his luck. He was corralled in a completely grassless small enclosure, surrounded by a barbed wire fence some four foot six inches high. The farm worker who met us at the farm gate gave us directions to find him, and said when he got hungry he would jump out and help himself to whatever he could find on the farm, leaving his companion mare to semi-starvation. He looked so poor but had the bearing of a real athletic type. He was no longer really rideable, so we brought him home and our farrier nearly expired when he saw his emaciated frame. However after good stable management and plenty of TLC on his poor old legs with Cider vinegar, within six months he attracted a lot of interest, for he was an outcross for Robert's daughters and at 15.3 hands suitable for breeding hunters and jumpers out of little thoroughbred mares.

Another big jumper was one of our pony stallions, Firestep bred by Miss Brook, a very well known New Forest breeder. He was bought in to use on Pickwick's daughters and at 13.2 hands was a flashy little fellow of real show-type. In the thirteen years we were at Lickfolds we accumulated two hundred acres of rented grazing land, in several different sites. Silverbeck at Churt was a thirteen-acre enclosure, behind a Victorian iron fence. My sons and students loathed this area, as we only managed to get hold of it as I guaranteed to clear it of the most ghastly shoulder-high crop of ragwort. Every single summer morning we piled into my Mini van and pulled one full load of weed, before coming home. As I pointed out to my bolshie team, the quicker they pulled it the sooner we could start on the day's chores. Working with horses has to be fun, but some unpleasant chores *must* be done.

Ultimately we cleared the whole thirteen acres, and eventually when a visiting rep. wanted to show how his new weed killer would deal with ragwort rosettes, he had a twenty-minute search to find one. In the winter we kept about a dozen pony mares down there, turned out with Firestep, and fed their hay on the sandy turf under the iron fence. As soon as Firestep heard us coming up the drive in the van, he would jump out and come to greet us; as I approached I would put my hand out of the van window and give the door a loud rap and tell him to get back in the field, he would immediately wheel round, canter off and jump back, nimble as a cat. He never tried to jump out at any other time and when we decided to geld him at the age of seven, as we had not enough work for him, we found him a lovely home with a schoolgirl who adored him. She would come home from school and jump on his back in his stable and consult him about her homework. She jumped him in pony classes with great success.

Pony peck orders are interesting. Feeding at the iron fence, the first one up would be the herd leader which was always Isobelle, then the peck order stretched down to the youngest filly. The stallion never ate with the mares, but stood back to see there was no fighting between the females, which he would punish immediately. We were very fortunate when a great friend of ours offered us Pickwick's beautiful black half-sister, Persuasion. She had bought her as a foal, and she was a first-class show-pony mare. However, in their nicely fenced small post and railed paddocks she had become overbearingly bossy to her very quality riding-pony stock and had caused some damage to the 'star'. I knew that we could not afford to buy this beautiful pony at her proper price and so she made me an offer we could not refuse.

Darling Perry came home with us, and later on at Olympia was reserve champion to her brother for the New Forest In-Hand Championship. She bred some sixteen foals with us, living to twenty-four years of age — but first she had to establish her peck order with the herd. It amazed me that for three days she took her place at head of the feed line, I could not believe Isobelle would tolerate this. On the fourth day Perry came in at eighth place — fortunately with no damage visible. Is would know better than that! Gradually she progressed up the peck order until she stood second to Is, and this was her place until the end of Isobelle's life at the age of thirty-four years.

Another interesting example of the instincts of stallions in the wild, was when a mare was added to the field numbers who had aborted a foal. She was examined by the Vet, and found completely clear, but Firestep kept her away from the herd for several weeks — just in case.

Many years later Fisherman ran with fifteen of our purebred Cleveland mares, high above the Exe Valley. We bought a mare in the Yorkshire Breed sales who came home to join his band. They all settled down fine until one day we found the poor mare beaten up and exiled from the band. Examination showed her to have a small vaginal discharge. She was brought home immediately for a vet examination, to find that she was harbouring enough virulent bugs to have finished our Cleveland breeding operation for ever. This resulted in cauterisation of the uterus, her use confined to riding only. Fisherman had looked after our interests.

Royal Show, 1983. Ramblers Bonita, two years,
Bolivia, her dam and new foal —
all first prize winners.

Wiscombe Arthur, sire of many champions
and a sensible ride

20

I still like to go up to Ascot sales and watch the thoroughbred stock go through the ring. You see so many different types of horses, from youngsters bred for the flat who failed to make the grade (as so many do), some can be a possibility for retraining as hacks or polo ponies, to the more substantial jumping types that can be recovered for point-to-pointing as well of course as the real McCoy nicely placed in the middle of the day which gets the bloodstock agents reaching for their phones whilst their clients listen to the bidding as it soars up often to be knocked down to overseas purchasers. It is I find fascinating to see the top trainers' assessment of working leg injuries — for many a bargain can be found amongst the battle-scarred veterans of the jumping game.

As we had such a lot of interest in our stallions, I felt we could really find some work for a good-looking thoroughbred stallion, and although our purse was very small, one very foggy November morning, we went up to the sales to find nobody had yet arrived through the murk to view what was on offer. We found

Werrion a very attractive chestnut — an early lot who had been raced on a number of occasions, but was unable to make anything of his chances being consistently second. His sire was Weepers Boy and his pedigree ran back to Gold Hill, a sire of Jumpers. He was a compact, strong little horse, originally trained by Balding. I believe his owner decided to try and train him himself and broke him down. He had been nursed back to health by a very professional lady who was known to the trainer. She had bought Werrion to the sale and told me she was sure he would be a suitable candidate for a stallion; the owners were going to stand him themselves but changed their mind.

Werrion was ours for four hundred pounds, he came home with us and was a real joker from the very first. When we got back I showed him to the students, and took off his travelling sheet and asked one of them for a blanket which I placed on his back — as they handed me his over-rug I made to put it on, only to find that he had removed the blanket on the off-side and was offering it back to me. He did the same with the roller as I held the rugs down and we all fell about laughing.

Later on Janet, a sweet little girl from Durham, took him on as her special charge. He had a lovely double-facing box of about twenty by twenty feet in size, and when she went looking for his tail bandage which he used to hide in the straw he would follow her around with a soppy expression on his face. When she gave up the search and went off to get another bandage, the missing one would be tossed over the door or on occasion dunked in the water bucket.

He was a great favourite with the students and fortunately also with our clients. We took him to the Hunters Improvement Society stallion Show at Newmarket in March. (Where Alan had to lead him as women were at that time not allowed to show their horses!) And he won a Premium for Surrey for which there had been no horse forward for some time. The Premium was his purchase price, four hundred pounds, and he took forty mares his first year which the HIS considered merely a 'start' because stallions in the scheme were expected to get between sixty and a hundred mares.

One of our hunting friends brought her daughter's little Connemara-cross mare to him when both daughters went to University. This service produced Myross who was subsequently a Gold Medalist at the Helsinki European Games. The rider was Lorna Clark; she must have been startled when the family refused an enormous price for him. Debby is our Vet today, and Myross was put down not so very long ago at twenty-seven.

The seventies were a very good time for horse-breeding, we had a string of foreign visitors coming to buy our home-bred New Forest stock, and also wanting nice young quality horses for dressage and jumping. We used to make regular visits up to Wetherby sales, held on the racecourse, and occasionally took Robert up to enter the King George Fifth Stallion Championship for the Cleveland stallion top honour. The trouble was that this was held in mid-April just when our stallions were becoming very busy and the long journey meant we did not want him faced with a backlog of mares on his return.

One year a coach load of French buyers came to see our New Forest ponies. We took them down to the out-fields where we had half a dozen beautiful Pickwick two and three year-olds running out. I was not pleased when they started making horrid dealer noises behind them, flapping their coats at them, trying to discern their quality I suppose, but not the sort of behaviour I liked to see. I showed my disapproval and told Alan quietly I wouldn't sell them anything — I was going home, and left him to cope.

Apparently my misgivings were noted by the buyers and I did not discuss the ponies at all as I handed out the tea and sandwiches to them as a polite British hostess should. Eventually after much discussion together their leader came to Alan and asked if any ponies were available. As I nodded, then asked them which were they interested in, they said *all* and I put a high price on them and we made a deal. The following year one of the fillies was made the French New Forest Champion.

Earlier in these jottings I mentioned my interest in Belted Galloways, a wonderful Scottish breed of cattle, with very easily identified markings in the shape of a large white belt encircling a lavish jet black coat of bear-like density (it is cold where these cattle hail from).

Rambler's Selina by Pickwick out of Rambler's Siesta which I have already referred to as a top JA junior jumper was entered for the Surrey County Show as a yearling. Some German clients of ours who we knew to be excellent pony breeders were very taken with her as she had won her class at Windsor; a price was mentioned which had to be confirmed by her husband when he came over for the Breed Show in August. Meanwhile she confirmed the lady's opinion by winning the Class and the Breed Championship at Surrey County.

If anything was asking for an unfavourable placing at the Breed Show this was it. However on this occasion all went well and she won her class and the Youngstock Championship and we sold her for seven hundred pounds. This does not sound much by today's standards, but it may surprise you to hear that by most extraordinary coincidence two weeks later we saw in the paper a herd of 'Belties' a very, very rare breed were to be sold at Reading market. I went up to the sale and was able to report to Alan on my return, that I had bought ten young pedigree in-calf cows, for the price of our New Forest filly.

The cattle were turned out on an outlying small farm that we rented. You cannot grow good grass for equines without grazing other livestock to keep grass sweet and parasites down. Sheep are very good for this job but the fencing required for them is often unsuitable for horses so that cattle are most popular for this job. The high-growing grasses kept down by the cattle, who ingest the equine parasites with no ill effects and whose own parasites, have no ill effect on the horses.

It was interesting to us to see how these semi-feral cattle conducted their daily life. They are a fiercely independent breed with a strong corporate responsibility for their offspring, so that they preferred to calve outside on their own, hiding their newborn calf in patches of weeds or undergrowth for the first few days as deer do also. It was necessary to keep a very sharp eye on their udders and vulvas (well masked by shaggy hair) to spot a freshly-calved cow. As all calves have to be ear-marked as soon after birth as possible, in practice with these shy protective cattle, we had to take the pick-up into the field, and driving very fast, pick up the calf and in the back of the truck, and at some speed, ear-tag it with the Ministry number, and a plastic herd ID, and get it back into its hiding place without being attacked by anxious Mum who would certainly do you no good if she could get at you whilst the calf was shouting for help.

Of course over the years, they became very used to our ways, and were quite unfazed by these operations, but dealing with a first calf heifer with a complicated calving was always a dicey job. In really severe snowy weather when other cattle were bawling at the barn door for bag food and forage, our 'girls' would gather round one of the big holly trees in their winter fields, and placing the calves inside under the lowest branches in shelter would lie down in a ring outside them, to keep the foxes and the draughts off.

When we had cows due to calve, I used to get up in the early dawn (because this is usually the preferred time for calving) and go round the cows to see if there was a new calf or signs of parturition. It was always unnerving to see the eyes of numerous foxes gleaming in my torch light waiting around, hopefully, drawn by the smell of birth, looking for after-births to eat, or a weak calf or careless mother. The farm was unfortunately too near suburbia for the hunt to be able to come and sort them out.

We made a long drive over to Kent to find an unrelated bull and were lucky enough to find a handsome quiet bull in Alexander. He soothed the girls' nervous fears and when it was necessary to move the stock onto new grazing or for them to go through the crush for handling, as leader he followed whichever of us was in front with the usual bait of cattle cobs, cattle-nuts made up into larger biscuits shaken about in a bucket.

Quite the nicest thing about this breed were the super Scottish Beltie enthusiasts who journeyed all the way down from their glens, to see our herd and encourage us. Mr Bernie, the Breed Secretary, gave me a grave lecture on handling Belties and instructed me: 'You must not be chasing them about with dogs, but let them adopt you, Mrs

Roberts.' I assured him that we would not be chasing them about, and it was he who suggested the cattle cobs.

One day passing George's school early one morning on Founders Day with the horsebox, we were horrified to see Alex and his wives on the sports ground, shortly to be the centre of activities and a mile away from where they should have been. Nipping into the front of the lorry we found the usual impedimenta used in travelling horses including a coloured plastic bucket, in which we put a couple of spanners to make a satisfactory noise, and then with one of us in front with the bucket, and one in the rear Alex took his wives quietly home again, leaving no trace of their visit.

The only people who hated the Belties were the Ministry Vets. The girls had only to spot a khaki Vet's overall and they took off or took over. Our own Vet testing a freshly calved cow himself suffered a near miss, losing his Wellingtons as he jumped clear of a charging mum who carried on to make a huge dent in a strong Victorian iron gate in the yard.

Though practised regularly the herd loathed going down to the yard, where we had a good cattle race in which they were confined for veterinary treatment. In time we built up a very good trade for our youngstock at the many rare breed parks being established all over the country. Alan used to deliver them all over the country, as it was difficult for me to be away from the stud, with two or three students and our own two sons to organise and feed. As I had no help in the house at all — keeping the house tidy was quite a job in itself. We made sure that there were always good hot meals for them to come into, as they lived as family with us.

New students would often come to us saying they did not eat cooked breakfasts, or ate only tiny portions of lunch. I never worried about this at all, but in the time-honoured way of any experienced feed-master, waited for them to get hungry. We all worked jolly hard and sharing meals together was fun — in no time they were back for second helpings. Lunch was the demarcation line between the morning chores and the pleasant afternoons where with the radio on in the tack room, grooming and leading out stallions and show youngsters, tack cleaning and tying up and handling foals and yearlings; as well a leaning-over and breaking youngsters were the high spots of the day. The evening feeds put up in bucket, waiting for the deadline of four thirty, before evening stables.

It was a very happy time for us all, and even now some forty years later we are in touch with some of our ex-lasses and their families — the lads however were not so good at keeping in touch — typical males — I often wonder where they are now.

Ramblers Lee Foundation mare and regular winner

James Stephenson, Secretary of the
Cleveland Bay Horse Society, presents Sonia
with the Female Championship Southern Show

21

We were very lucky that throughout our stud career, we were able to call on the services of several first-class stud Vets. So we were able to obtain up to date treatment of difficult mares. As at that time there were no ultrasonic scanners, it was imperative to have a really top professional to palpate the mares for early pregnancy which we needed at twenty-one days or so. Owners naturally wanted their mares home again as soon as possible, and so even if the mare refused the stallion, when carefully teased, it was important to have a second informed opinion. I must say that in many ways I considered these top men to be superior to a scanner — they were practically never wrong, and were equally good at finding twins. Of course their hands were kept very sensitive in the summer as they concentrated on this job exclusively.

The only difficulty was that in a really popular practice, there are many studs competing for their services. On a Vet day in mid-season, every box on the stud filled with mares, and so impossible to muck out the very messy summer grass droppings mounting up every hour, the endless waiting for a late Vet to come in was a fearful pain, since all the mares had to be returned to different fields when the work was finished. The Staff would be doing a lot of clock-watching if they were going out that night.

Showing in the summer was very difficult if we were busy, and we made a point of never staying away the night if we could help, it being our opinion (as many trainers also agree) that horses never really rest away from home, the sooner they are back again in their own stable the better. We never used show tap water if we could find room for a churn of our own, as horses hate strange water particularly that from temporary hoses and taps on a showground.

The covering of mares was always priority, and was never carried out by anyone but Alan and I. On one occasion we had a very nice thoroughbred mare visiting which had been barren the previous season. Her owner explained that his Vet had discovered that she was only ready to cover for a very short period of a few hours, as her responses were un-synchronised. We undertook to get her covered properly by Werrion, but I suppose that it was inevitable that she should show strong signs of oestrus on the day the native pony classes were held at the South of England Show. We felt that we had a good chance with Pickwick and so started in good time with the covering.

It was an incredibly hot summer's day, and the mare was exceedingly capricious, so that with the stallion covered in sweat, we told the girls that we should not be going to the show after all as it was getting so late. In due course we succeeded in getting a really good service, and mopping our brows we put Werrion away. The girls who took over the mare from us for her to be walked and grazed in-hand both knew that we were both looking forward to going to Ardingly, and told us: 'We've cut your sandwiches, groomed Pickwick and he is loaded up in the lorry. Hurry up. You'll just make it!' We were rewarded later in the day by winning the Mountain and Moorland Championship and being the first New Forest Wembley Qualifier, and have a crystal decanter with the Lloyds Black Horse to prove it.

After Philip had had two seasons experience with Mrs Powell, he showed interest in coming home to help me with the stud. Alan was increasingly busy with his NFU work, so his help was welcome. We had boy students at the time, as well as girls, so some jollying up by a male of their own age group was a good idea, and any of the lads skiving in the loo whilst we were busy mucking-out was given short shrift.

The only thing about having Phil back with us was that we had to have his stallion too. This was Romancero whose debut in the Larkspur Derby had caused confusion when he came down at Tattenham Corner causing an unfortunate collision. He was a very beautiful classically-bred dark bay horse; he was loaned to us to give him a good home. He was over seventeen hands, with the most enormous front, so all the electrical wiring in the roof of Werrion's box which had been annexed by Phil because of his size, had to be protected from the ravages of his teeth.

The two main snags with him were first a leisurely attitude over equine love life — the covering team had to take a newspaper to read in the covering yard he was so slow, and his mares were bored with his very lukewarm conduct. The other snag was that once out of his stable, it could take ages to get him back again. Life on a stud with several stallions in mid-season has to be extremely well-regulated to get all the in-season mares covered, walked and returned to their fields. Foaling mares watched all night, visiting foals taught to lead. It was not long before I felt that Phil's protégée was the last straw, and vowed that his was to be a short stay with us.

During the winter we still found time to enjoy our hunting. When Ray Stovold, our master, hung up his boots after twenty-five years as MFH, it was sad that as our hunt country had been loaned by the Chiddingfold and Leconfield Hunt, together with the Surrey Union Hunt at the time this wartime pack was set-up under his mastership, that upon his retirement there was some pressure from these two hunts, to return the loaned country which was specific to this mastership, and as by then their own hunting area had been reduced greatly by urban sprawl.

Our own farmers were furious at this event, as they rightly pointed out, the hunt country was their own farmland and they felt that they had been overlooked in this archaic apportioning of 'Hunt Country', to these senior hunts. Alan was unique in holding an all-Branch meeting of the NFU to discuss their disapproval of the dissolution of the Farmers' Hunt, and tremendous efforts were made to bring in a new Master, and keep the hunt viable. But under heavy pressure — some of it from the retiring Master — the problem of the loaned country could not be resolved. Sadly the Chiddingfold Farmers' Hunt was disbanded, and a very healthy sum left in perpetuity to the Hunt Pony Club which flourishes today. Our hunt-members joined either the Surrey Union, or Chiddingfold and Leconfield, now merged of course with the Cowdrey Hunt.

As we were now living on the Hampshire border, Mr Ken Goschens' private pack of hounds were in a similar position to our last pack, loaned country by the Hampshire Hunt of which he was previously master, and also some from the Chiddingfold and Leconfield. He and his wife had built up a beautiful uniform pack of hounds over many years, and we were invited to join them, together with a handful of other privileged supporters. Of course some of the country was farmed by Alan's NFU members and were old friends of ours, also now, the hunt country extended south toward Petersfield.

We had some wonderful days with Mr and Mrs Goschen and their huntsman, Ted Rafton. It was very interesting to see another pack of hounds at work, using a different technique. These hounds were particularly quick to inform one another when a reliable hound spoke, and using their own initiative would run like light — close under the proverbial blanket formation. It was very impressive.

Mrs 'Wanni' Goschen, immaculately mounted on quality hunters, was a charming and effective field master, her husband hunting hounds with Ted. They were supported both at home and in the field by Jackie and Grace, who looked after them with great devotion. There was a great team of hunt supporters and a very happy atmosphere, resulting in a definite reduction in predatory foxes.

At the same time our own business was getting too much for me to manage without Alan's help. As we were getting older we decided that we would pass on our Beltie cattle quite lucratively to the rare breed enthusiasts and start up in South Devons, the largest British beef breed, which I had learned to milk as a child when they were always then ticketed as dual-purpose — the Devon farmers milking the cows for several months after calving, and then allowing them to suckle or double-suckle their calves with or without an extra calf, out at grass.

South Devons are quiet, calm and easy to handle, we did not have to be so active to manage them. They were always called the M'dears and needed only an encouraging 'C'up C'up M'dear' to quietly file in whatever direction they were needed. They had huge calves which were not always so cooperative as they got older, so our Border collies, who had been kept away from the Belties and taught to be very quiet and gentle when keeping naughty foals up the mares' sides, had to be retrained to keep all the calves up with the cows when we moved the herd about, or the stroppy bull calves could cause mayhem with the herd's progress.

When Alan resigned his position with the NFU, all his Branches gave him a terrific send-off, and many of his members have remained friends to this day. In fact the heavy responsibilities of his job, which included a large number of evening meetings had begun to affect his health, and at one time we had a nasty scare about his sight, which fortunately turned out to be only stress-induced.

In the course of setting up our new herd, we regularly went to the South Devon sales at Exeter, and once again found so many charming friends amongst the top breeders. Tom Wilcox from Modbury was happy to sell us some heifer calves, and Alan used to drive down to their lovely farm in the South Hams, the fields running down to the sea and their private beach, and bring the calves back in a hired van. When Mrs Wilcox asked what time he would be down, she was startled when he replied, 'In time for breakfast, my dear.' She had a look of disbelief when he pooped his horn to announce his arrival at eight a.m. just in time for a real farmer's breakfast.

Apart from the beef herd we made quite a lot of hay and also baled and carted straw from some of the big arable farmers in Hampshire. The Cleveland Bays were building up and we were reducing the Forest ponies to a small nucleus, from which colts could be sold.

We had some forty-five acres of old pasture adjoining Lickfolds farm on which our breeding mares ran in the summer. It was quite a long walk for me before breakfast to see some thirty mares and affix head collars on those showing signs of oestrus, so that the students coming along later, would know which to bring up for trying to the stallions. To help in this chore we had a good little Firestep two-year-old gelding, which the vet implanted in the neck with a testosterone capsule. He ran with the bunch and was always to be found with any in-season mares so it made their selection easy. He was never too coltish nor would he make a nuisance of himself, so he was a favourite of the mares.

It was interesting to note that if you run horses in really large bunches on open ground, you never have any bullying or scrapping. The newcomers circle the bunch for a few days until they are allowed to enter by the boss mares, and then calmly take their place with the hierarchy, very similar to horses running the prairies or the Asian steppes. At the end of the season the gelding had his capsule removed — or what was left of it — and settled into normal winter hibernation. His temper was always sweet and he later made a lovely riding pony like his dad.

In 1975 we started having hot summers. That year was hot enough for those who have to do physical work, but the following year the temperatures were terrific. We had three students at the time and four stallions in use. Robert had fifty mares, and Werrion over forty, Pickwick and his son, Prince Picolo, were also in use. No matter how you try to regulate the number of mares coming in season on a given day, one hot, sunny day in May and June, will have every empty mare in the stud in season, which makes a considerable demand on the stallions. If it continues to be very hot and sunny some of those who have already been covered successfully at the previous heat will also return in a semi-heat and cause additional nuisance and unnecessary work to get them all tried to the stallion or teaser successfully.

Of course these days the studs using chilled semen for AI and copious Vet work have things much easier, but in the seventies, customers had a fit if they had a Vet fee of more than twenty pounds, and so our Vets would swab all visiting mares onto sealed plates, which we would culture ourselves in an ingenious adaptation of a metal bread bin and an EL light bulb — with a thermometer to check the temperature. We cultured every swab very satisfactorily, and at the first sign of any growth, the plate was rushed up to the Vet surgery well-wrapped, for them to check the nature of the bacteria, and return on the next vet visit to wash out the mare with the relevant antibiotic. Of course it was by these methods we were able to keep our customers' expenses down, and encourage them to breed regularly from injured or elderly mares of quality, which would otherwise have to be put down.

During the 1976 heat wave we had regular temperature in our yard of over 90 degrees, sometimes this had hardly abated by eight o'clock at night. Because of this we used to turn Robert out in a lovely high, breezy paddock two miles down the road for the night, after covering his last mare. At six in the morning we would bring him home to cover his first mare of the day whilst it was still cool. Werrion as a thoroughbred could stand the heat rather better, so he was in at night, covering before breakfast. At lunch-time, if any mares had to be covered, this was done before lunch, and then all the stallions were stood under a cold hose to cool off before their feeds.

The family and staff all had their lunch under the old apple tree on the lawn, but in the 90s it was so hot it was difficult to enjoy your food. Alan and I would cover the last mares at 9.30 p.m., just before taking Robert up to his eyrie for the night. Before long all the pastures were burned up. Visitors from India flying into Heathrow said India looked green in comparison to the south of England. You would have expected the mares' condition to have deteriorated, however, horses do really well in hot sunshine on high exposed ground. Flies do not like dry heat, and burning sun keeps the pastures free of parasites. There was ample clean water (the students doing their regular summer afternoon excursion round the troughs, with scrubbing brushes and balers) the horses all looked marvellous, as did the staff, only I found the burning summer was weakening me, and in late June a pony kick on the front of my left shin from an unshod pony, began to give me grave problems.

As I limped around my duties making endless meals, I began to think how nice it would be for Alan and I to take early retirement and together find some little place in Devon and get some peace from the endless work of a public stud. We had been thirteen years at Lickfolds and got it into pretty good shape, the additional land was all rented so that the capital value of the main property should buy us a smaller place for us to take our Clevelands and South Devons.

As I tried to get some help with my damaged leg, every time I was fixed to see the orthopaedic consultant, in late summer there was difficulty because of the holiday period. Finally my GP who had done his very best for me from the start, got me down to the new Scanning Department at Southampton, then in its infancy, and it was clear that there was infection in the bone, but the Consultant considered it best to leave it alone and hope that it would clear itself.

Alan who was worried for me also, fell in with my suggestions that we should take things easier — we had had a tiresome summer with our teenage crew, and were at our very lowest. We put Lickfolds in the market and sold immediately although with a lengthy completion date, and started another phase. It was however fortunate that I could not look ahead and see the pain and misery that my quite trifling accident would cause me, and that it would eventually be five years later, before I was able to give up the heavy antibiotic medication necessary after severe osteomyelitis followed an unsuccessful operation the following year at Taunton, and my saviours at the Nuffield Hospital in Oxford, had removed a third of the bone in my left fib to save my leg.

Ramblers Leonie breed champion Royal Show

R Leah and R Lucky Miss, property of
HM The Queen, put to the Balmoral Sociable
at the CB display, Dunster Castle

22

There are some periods in a lifetime which it is too painful to remember. Our move to a picture-book little farm on the Redlands of the Exe valley, where with the traditional Cob farmhouse set in a sheltered bowl, our fields sloping up some hundreds of feet. The view of our South Devons running with their bull in one direction, and Fisherman and some fifteen Cleveland Bay mares on the top fields will always stay in my memory, as will the sixteen-point red deer stag and his wives enjoying making a hash of our ready-to-cut hay field — so very beautiful in their transgressions. There was an enormous population of hares on the farm. They would settle down at night on the sides in a hull-down position, only their enormous ears silhouetted in the failing light, from the windows of the house.

Extra land was rented by us on the other side of the Exe, but after an abortive operation at Taunton Hospital, my leg was agonising and it was obviously going from bad to worse. Eventually there was talk of a further operation, but I was pretty sure certain that amputation was on the cards. My sister in Oxford managed to arrange for me to see a famous orthopaedic surgeon at the Nuffield, Oxford, who had been recommended to her. When we got up there he viewed the depleted number of X-rays that we had had the greatest difficulty in extracting from the Taunton Hospital with a wry smile — he had seen it all before. He agreed to take me in on the National Health, as he felt that such severe osteomyelitis would be an interesting challenge for his Team, as this was a teaching hospital. There would be a considerable wait for a National Health bed, so to give it a chance I was to use a day bed, and keep the leg well above my head for as long as it would take to get me a bed. He understood that as smallholders we had no funds for a private operation.

The three weeks I waited were appalling, and though I had made some friends with some lovely Devon ladies, I was mostly on my own whilst Alan was busy on the farm, although Jim, one of our students, had come down with us. On one occasion after Jim had gone home, Alan was harrowing one of our steep fields, with our new John Deere tractor. From my couch I saw the tractor go out of control downhill, its wheels apparently turning backwards as it shot past my viewing point, and I was sure that it had turned over on Alan — an all too frequent occurrence in that part of the world, as he did not reappear. I could not walk to see if he was okay and the telephone was out of order, so this was the most agonising experience of my life. Eventually Alan turned up, having decided the job was unsafe, and put the tractor away.

Once at the Nuffield I tried to clear my mind of troubles, and had a moving experience. Whilst I was awaiting my operation one of the other patients had gathered a small prayer group of her visitors together. As she was encased in a steel, back and neck brace, I called her Joan of Arke. It was a bright moonlight autumn night. I believe that this ward had once been used as a tuberculosis sanatorium so it was incredibly light and airy having roof-lights which were uncurtained. Fixing my eyes on the beautiful moon I felt a sensation of peace and kindness directed at me. I had no idea at the time that these good people were trying to help me, only the sensation of calm acceptance; although sleep was impossible during the night I was uplifted to a degree I have never experienced before and refused sleeping pills from the night staff.

I have heard of out-of-the-body experiences in more recent years, but in those days if people experienced them, they kept quiet in case they were considered nutcases! However during my very long operation, at some time I looked down on my body on the operating table from a great height and was joined by my brother Richard who had died many years before, and also my old family friend Olive — she of the good ship Bolivia whom I have mentioned before, who had died more recently. I was very pleased to see them and we started to travel down a long dark corridor, with sunlight at the far end. However the sun soon faded away and I felt a deep sense of loss as my two companions left me and I heard someone trying to wake me up.

I was very lucky to have got to this wonderful hospital and the Senior Consultant, a tough little Aberdonian, allowed me to have my bed taken out to the Grounds in the fine autumn weather. A long-suffering Ward Sister arranging for help to push it out and when the Professor and his team of acolytes did the ward tours, they all came out to see me ensconced outside, with much murmuring from the younger men who turned up their collars and looked overcome with cold. Sister was very concerned that I might get chilled, but I explained to her that for me to be in a hot stuffy atmosphere was as bad for me as for her city patients to have to endure the cold of a wet winter day outside on the farm.

She was a lovely lady and always had a sherry in a medicine cup for Alan who got up every week to see me from Devon, a difficult journey when he had so much to do, and it was very fortunate that he had our youngest son, George, who had returned home to help him. I was chained to my bed in plaster for four weeks, but eventually after having a calliper fitted to my shoe by the prosthetics department, I was allowed home supported by heavy medication of Fucidin to wait the long period necessary to grow new, clean bone, one third of the main fib. having been removed.

Some five years later I was able to discard my old friend the calliper. Truly a miracle in a woman over fifty years old and having been given only a fifty, fifty chance. The Fucidin medication lasted for nearly five years. The Prof. said that they had previously had only one man on a long-term Fucidin — but he had died before they could analyse the effect on the system. I however kept quite well on the stuff and kept clear of colds and flu which would normally have laid me low.

After my hospital internment I had to be near enough to Oxford to attend out-patients clinics. Alan and George, who had made numerous improvements to the Devon farm, sold it very satisfactorily, sending the cattle and brood mares back to Philip who had bought one of our small rented farms. We found a smallholding with some potential, and a lovely warm house with a good central heating system, close to Farnham and we started what was to prove an extremely cold snowy winter in reasonable comfort. Eventually after Alan converted existing buildings into more stables, we got our mares and cattle back from Phil who was glad to have the extra space to build up his own herd of Friesians. Within a year I was feeling quite strong again.

Percy Podger found me a dear little grey Cob to carry me, and Alan got very ingenious in altering all my footwear to take a calliper, from evening sandals to hunting boot, though I had to be careful not to fall off, or get the tree branches hooked up in the calliper whilst hunting, with the previous year called a 'no tax year' because of my health.

Alan was now Secretary of the National Pony Society — a post now entitled Executive-Secretary, his experience with running NFU branches very useful in this his new appointment. He took over the office papers in literally a couple of shoeboxes from his predecessor, who had run the office from his home in Basingstoke and set up a new office in Alton which seemed to be a suitable centre for most southern members' convenience; with some experienced staff who were also new to the job, Alan was in his element.

Once again I was on my own with the horses and found Karen, a local school-leaver, who lived close by and came to us for training, making herself so indispensable she ended up as head girl and is still, a dear friend owning some of my most cherished Cleveland Bay mares.

It was the greatest good fortune for us that the large estate up the road, Bushy Lease, had been sold and the new owner decided to keep the big house and sell on the farm and most of the land. Eventually we managed to exchange our smallholding for what we now renamed Lea Farm, and once again we had a decent-sized property around us together with our Clevelands, South Devons and New Forest ponies which had been out on lease during the period of my illness.

A little conversion was carried out on the magnificent estate buildings to give us a staff flat in the granary, a good tack-room and eventually a lovely conversion of the big double-row cow sheds into a large bungalow with views all over the farm. At this time we had a number of students and were regular exhibitors at the Royal Show with our Clevelands. We also had a big Open Day for the Cleveland Bay Southern Breeders Club, sponsored by BHF Feeds. This took a lot of organising as this Club which Alan and I had instigated originally, had grown in numbers as there were by now a number of pure-bred stallions standing in the south and west of the country. These were mainly being used on thoroughbred or quality type mares to get big upstanding jumping or eventing types.

One of our student's fathers was Catering Instructor to the Ghurkha regiment stationed just up the road at Church Crookham. They took on a few extra private catering jobs and were able to give us a marvellous quote for supplying us with a fork lunch for over two hundred visitors, served on the terrace of the newly completed bungalow, the stallions and breeding stock paraded below in view of the guests. Also included was a judging competition of six pure-bred mares. The Ghurkhas excelled themselves and we had an enormous spread and lived on the leftovers for days afterwards.

Alan attending Ascot Paddocks for the Dartmoor Society Show in his NPS role, reported on what a wonderful site this would be for us to hold a Southern Cleveland Bay Show. As all the breed shows (other than those at the Royal) were held in Yorkshire, the huge distances involved in travelling these very large horses to a northern show prevented many enthusiasts from showing their own stock, or seeing other people's, which is equally interesting.

Eventually (not without some difficulties) the main Society agreed we could go ahead and try and get a show going in the south, and Alan and I organised classes for both pure and part-breeds. For the first year or two we, and Marygold Nixey, the only other large breeder in the south, used to have to take two or three lorry loads each up to Ascot on the day, to keep up the numbers, particularly in the youngstock classes. It was jolly hard work on top of the other show organising required, and neither Marygold nor us were sorry when numbers gradually built up and we were able to take smaller numbers. We used to hold our AGM in the lads' hostel the night before combined with some social activities and refreshments. It was great to see a big contingent from the West Country as well as the southerners all having a good time. Of course the facilities at Ascot are marvellous, so to have first class stabling for these big horses and also catering facilities was great.

The paddocks themselves proved a wonderful background for this truly British breed, and we had quite a lot of foreign visitors drop-in to see the show although not nearly enough to subsidise our show. However Ascot being a royal property HM The Queen who is a Patron of the breed and herself a breeder of Cleveland Bays which are used at the Mews, saw to it that we were given special terms and INTERVET generously sponsored us for many years.

Ramblers Lottie, owned by HM The Queen.
Winner of innumerable breed championships,
with Alan at the Royal Show.

Alan and Sonia at the August NPS Show, 1978

23

There has always been a small market abroad for the finest Cleveland stock which seem to flourish in countries with climates very different from our own. Soon after getting to Lea Farm, rather nearer to civilisation again, I heard that the Japanese were looking for another stallion. Rambler's Reform, a son of Robert out of a great old mare we had purchased from the Sinclairs, had been broken in during our brief spell in Devon by our dressage instructor friend, Annaleise Johnson. He was a really gentle young stallion with an enormous jump, (having popped over the five foot six school doors for a lark). We now had another really good colt from April-Love by Fisherman called Rambler's Renown, so we offered Reform to the Japanese.

This time they sent the Director of the Imperial stud, together with two interpreters from Saatchi and Saatchi as the Director who was about to retire after long service with the Imperial stud, could speak no English and as the Director of Rambler's stud could speak no Japanese, it was felt that interpreters would be sorely needed. I found the Director to be a charming chap, and despite our linguistic problems we could understand each other perfectly and were in fact several sentences in front of the interpreters who knew nothing of horses whatever, but had brought a camera to provide positive proof of the size of Reform's breeding equipment, and also of his satisfactory arousal when a mare was brought up to 'try' to him. After the soft porn, while our visitor was with us, I asked why I had heard nothing of the Clevelands they had bought from us some years before. Other countries, I said, who bought our stock kept us informed as to their progress. I was deeply disappointed and did not want this lovely young horse to disappear into a void where I never heard any more of him again. 'What,' I asked, 'happened to old horses in Japan?'

This approach concerned my visitor greatly, he earnestly brought out of his wallet a photograph of his own riding horse kept at the stud at the ripe old age of forty years. It certainly looked as cosseted as ours. He told me that similar to our own Royal Mews, the Emperor's horses were never resold but put down in old age as our own Mews horses are. He promised that if his superiors sanctioned the purchase of Reform, his son who was an

English scholar would send me regular reports on the British horses and report their breeding and progeny growth for me. I heard shortly afterwards that they were buying Reform and that he would be flying out straight away.

The Director was true to his word and sent me photos and statistics of all the British-bred Clevelands and all the subsequent foals and the arrangements for exercising, covering and general care. This information was arranged in a delightful handbook with Japanese calligraphy as well as the logistics in English. Some of the earlier horses which Marygold Nixey had exported, were still going strong at over twenty years of age, for the Imperial stud is situated at a high altitude well away from Tokyo's pollution so the stock enjoyed a healthy lifestyle. Later he reported to me sadly of his retirement which involved living far away from his beloved horses, but he asked his successor to continue sending me pictures and info.

April Love's next youngest son, Rambler's Caliph, went out to Australia. Her lovely Colt by Fisherman 'Renown' was bought by the late Lady Townshend. She sent him out to her Arabian stud in the USA to breed international-standard driving horses from Arabian mares. This he certainly succeeded in doing as Mr Charles Mathieson from Virginia drives many of these in his coaches and drags today. Eventually after Lady Townshend's death, Lord Townshend leased Renown now aged twelve years and previously hardly ridden, to Tom and Marilyn Webster at Idle Hour stud PA.

They imported about a dozen pure-bred fillies from us, among which we were able to include many different bloodlines. It was not long before Marilyn was competing at Lexington in cross-country and jumping and dressage, as well as the pure-breds appearing out hunting and it was not too long before we sent out Rambler's Richard Lionheart and Rambler's Lorenzo as different family lines.

It was of course so typical that as far as we were concerned we had the best quality young Clevelands ready for sale in the early eighties just when Margaret Thatcher had promised to look after the small businesses. In the UK we had the most appalling recession and decent horse sales were on the floor. We were standing six stallions at the time, including two pony stallions, and money was short. Rather unfortunately this coincided with Alan's rebellion against petticoat rule in the NPS and although it was difficult for us, I saw his point of view and when he gave his notice in, I had to think quickly to find a money-spinner.

In the event I looked around the Farnham, Odiham, Fleet area to see if there would be an opening for a small children's riding school — most of the equitation establishments would not take children until they were ten or twelve years old. We had a very suitable little open-span barn and concrete roads winding all round the farm buildings and yards. Such young children would have to be very carefully looked after in case of accident and also it all had to be great fun, so I went to Reading horse-sales and investigated all local sources of reliable out-grown ponies for lease to good homes, and found eight little ponies, four of which were large Shetlands. We gave the children half-hour lessons in the school followed by mounted games and Pony Club mounted exercises. In no time I had an enthusiastic clientele.

Our girl students would be schooling sixteen- to seventeen-hand Clevelands and then get down to sitting on and schooling nicely, the little riding school ponies, who could give them a lesson in sticking on at a buck, when the head and neck in front of you disappeared from sight. The children and the ponies and trainees loved it, and we had plenty of leaders on Saturday mornings, when we had two sessions. On Sundays our staff went home so I had to confine the teaching to the barns, so no pony could make off with a passenger rider. By Sunday afternoons I was so tired I could hardly walk, and had some sympathy — hitherto lacking — for teachers whinging about their exhausting, nine to three-thirty working day.

I found the effort of making things fun, with a lot of hilarious jollity very exhausting, and parents had a habit of coming back very late to pick pupils up, so we had to entertain them longer than was strictly fair. However they were such a lovely crowd and I was very touched that the children brought me presents. Our students were simply great about helping me, so it was a very happy, satisfying experience. It also helped us over a bad recession.

Alan was baling up straw all over the surrounding Hampshire arable, and had a terrific system of borrowed trailers stationed on the arable plains, where he would use the flat eight grab on the front-end loader to load the trailers, then from a precarious height climb-down and load another trailer, leaving the loaded trailers all over the area until the end of the day, when Phil with whatever drivers and tractors he could scrounge would come and help drive the procession home. With the help of the elevator, which I usually fed, the several barns we had were filled to overflowing. We had twenty-five stables and some fifty head of cattle to house, so haymaking and straw carting was a big physical effort.

Eventually the recession eased, but a lot of our money was tied up in this big place. Horse prices were still poor, but suddenly property prices seemed to be taking off — we were by then very used to assessing property fluctuations, so we asked a big figure for this very desirable property and were once again able to feel solvent, after a good sale.

All our working life we were lucky to be able to use a good private mortgage arranged by our solicitor. However it was at 14 per cent interest — but no repayment. This therefore necessitated a pretty regular turnover as agriculture and equiculture do not give big returns on such a small scale. It was very tedious therefore when our farming friends would say, 'What moving again' in a deprecating voice — when they had been lucky enough to inherit a working farm from their family. Sometimes we wondered if we should have taken on a big tenancy, but as farming incomes have plummeted, those of our friends with big rented farms around them were some of the first to get into financial trouble, as the agricultural depression began to bite. Fortunately the capital value of farmhouses and unwanted agricultural heritage buildings, however humble, have continued to rise, and never more so than in the south and west of the country.

However, needs must, when the devil drives; we had great satisfaction in improving our properties, many of which we had taken on in a very poor state. Alan could take on so many different jobs, from plumbing to house-building, or farm engineering. I in my way could wear many different hats. Life was never boring, but sometimes incredibly hectic.

With both our sons now married and living in the Exmoor National Park, we decided that the time was ripe for semi-retirement, and finding a comfortable bungalow in the Brendon Hills, and sixty acres of good grassland, just a few miles away from the boys, we started out on our last great adventure. Despite one rather severe heart attack, within two years of moving, Alan not only enjoyed regular hunting, but had been asked to take on the duties of Hunt Secretary again. It was a second heart attack some years later which indicated that full retirement was now the order of the day . . .

We do hope that you have enjoyed reading this large print book.

Did you know that all of our titles are available for purchase?

We publish a wide range of high quality large print books including:
Romances, Mysteries, Classics
General Fiction
Non Fiction and Westerns

Special interest titles available in large print are:
The Little Oxford Dictionary
Music Book
Song Book
Hymn Book
Service Book

Also available from us courtesy of Oxford University Press:
Young Readers' Dictionary
(large print edition)
Young Readers' Thesaurus
(large print edition)

For further information or a free brochure, please contact us at:
Ulverscroft Large Print Books Ltd.,
The Green, Bradgate Road, Anstey,
Leicester, LE7 7FU, England.
Tel: (00 44) 0116 236 4325
Fax: (00 44) 0116 234 0205

Other titles published by
The House of Ulverscroft:

MOVING MOUNTAINS

Claire Bertschinger

In Ethiopia in 1984, Claire Bertschinger, an International Red Cross nurse, was filmed surrounded by thousands of starving people and with limited supplies. She had the terrible task of choosing which children to feed, knowing that those she turned away might not last the night. Those shocking pictures inspired Bob Geldof; and, ultimately, Live Aid . . . Twenty years later Michael Buerk, whose television reports first showed those pictures, persuaded Claire to return to Ethiopia. Claire had always been haunted by the memory of having to make such terrible choices, but the survivors, calling her 'Mamma Claire', welcomed her back with open arms.

THE TERMINAL MAN

Sir Alfred Mehran and Andre Donkin

Mehran Karimi Nasseri, better known as 'Sir Alfred', has been living in the departure lounge of Terminal 1 of Charles de Gaulle Airport, Paris, for sixteen years. He sleeps on a bench, dines at McDonalds, and is surrounded by piles of magazines and his extensive diary. He arrived at the airport on 8th August 1988, intending to take a plane to London. Without the proper documentation he quickly found himself trapped in a bureaucratic catch-22 nightmare. Fearing arrest as an illegal immigrant if he left the terminal building, he has been waiting while lawyers and government officials argued about his case. This is his incredible story in his own words.

THE SKY SUSPENDED

Jim Bailey

While studying at Oxford University in the warm summer of 1939, Jim Bailey knew that war with Germany was looming. From a world of books and words, the nineteen-year-old saw that this was his moment to grasp something more real and, despite his fear of combat, he signed up to train as a pilot for the Royal Air Force and defend his country. Bailey flew fighters throughout World War II, from the Battle of Britain through Gibraltar and the Anzio beach-head to the landing in the South of France. This is the true story of youthful heroism and survival against the odds.